DAVID B. BURRELL, Hesburgh
Professor emeritus at University of Notre
Dame, teaches Ethics and Development
at Uganda Martyrs University. He has
published extensively in comparative
issues in philosophical theology in
Judaism, Christianity, and Islam and is
the·author of *Faith and Freedom* (2006),
Wiley-Blackwell.

D0992113

Towards a
Jewish-Christian-Muslim
Theology

Challenges in Contemporary Theology

Series Editors: Gareth Jones and Lewis Ayres
Canterbury Christ Church University College, UK and University of Durham, UK

Challenges in Contemporary Theology is a series aimed at producing clear orientations in, and research on, areas of "challenge" in contemporary theology. These carefully coordinated books engage traditional theological concerns with mainstreams in modern thought and culture that challenge those concerns. The "challenges" implied are to be understood in two senses: those presented by society to contemporary theology, and those posed by theology to society.

Published

Towards a Jewish-Christian-Muslim Theology

David B. Burrell

WILEY-BLACKWELL

A John Wiley & Sons, Ltd., Publication

This edition first published 2011
© 2011 John Wiley and Sons Ltd

Wiley-Blackwell is an imprint of John Wiley & Sons, formed by the merger of Wiley's global Scientific, Technical and Medical business with Blackwell Publishing.

Registered Office
John Wiley & Sons Ltd, The Atrium, Southern Gate, Chichester, West Sussex, PO19 8SQ, United Kingdom

Editorial Offices
350 Main Street, Malden, MA 02148-5020, USA
9600 Garsington Road, Oxford, OX4 2DQ, UK
The Atrium, Southern Gate, Chichester, West Sussex, PO19 8SQ, UK

For details of our global editorial offices, for customer services, and for information about how to apply for permission to reuse the copyright material in this book please see our website at www.wiley.com/wiley-blackwell.

The right of David B. Burrell to be identified as the author of this work has been asserted in accordance with the UK Copyright, Designs and Patents Act 1988.

Library of Congress Cataloging-in-Publication data is available for this book

HB: 9780470657553

A catalogue record for this book is available from the British Library.

This book is published in the following electronic formats:
ePDFs 9781444395785; Wiley Online Library 9781444395808;
ePub 9781444395792

Set in 10.5/13.5 pt Palatino by Toppan Best-set Premedia Limited, Hong Kong
Printed and bound in Singapore by Fabulous Printers Pte Ltd

1   2011

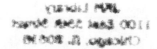

To a friend of more than half a century, Nikos Stavroulakis, animator of Etz Hayyim synagogue in Hania in Crete, who epitomizes the hospitality described in this study

Contents

Preface

While preparing to compose this study, I was privileged to spend the Jewish high holydays at Hania with my friend Nikos Stavroulakis in the Etz Hayyim synagogue (www.etz-hayyim-hania.org/). I had been overwhelmed by the rapprochement between Christian and Muslims at various levels effected since Pope Benedict's speech at Regensburg in 2006. His ill-advised example, apparently in homage to a one-time colleague at the university, distracted from a recondite thesis on the role reason has to play in elaborating religious tradition, eliciting an astutely critical response from 38 Muslim scholars within a month. And a year later, a carefully constructed document, entitled (from the Qur'an) *A Common Word between Us*, precipitated an exchange unprecedented in the last fourteen centuries. Something had happened, not without astute guidance, which called for a reassessment of the commonalities between these two often estranged traditions. I felt prepared and called to undertake such an inquiry, since my own work over the past quarter century had been focused on exchanges extant among Jews, Christians, and Muslims. Yet mesmerized by these recent events, I initially demurred from a triadic approach, lamely suggesting that monitoring actual or potential encounters between Christianity and Islam might at best be supplemented with links to Jewish tradition, while suggesting that these best remain illustrative, since Christianity and Islam are faith-traditions in a way that Judaism can be, but need not be. Yet while there is something right about that statement, it can also be grossly insulting, as celebrating the high holydays at Etz Hayyim synagogue forcibly reminded me.[1]

Yet I confess my initial *faux pas* here precisely to remind myself and recall to others how deeply Christian faith has been nourished in Jewish tradition from its beginning, illustrated whenever the New Testament refers to "the Scriptures" (that is, Hebrew Scripture), yet how easily the descriptor "Christian" can elide that originary fact. Even more personally, my own initiation into the mystery and fruits of dialog began with a celebrated mentor in Jerusalem, Marcel Dubois, OP, who spiced my initiation into the "sacred geography" of the Holy Land with trenchant reminders of a profoundly Jewish Jesus, best recovered through intercourse with living and believing Jews. Now the binary title – "Muslim-Christian theology" – can easily obscure that constitutive fact of Christian spiritual life and intellectual practice, so we begin with a proper Muslim *silsala*, giving due homage to mentors from all three Abrahamic traditions. So this elucidation of latent points of contact between Christians and Muslims, in selected theological topics over the centuries, will duly illustrate how that conversation regularly involved Jewish interlocutors as well. Our indispensable guide to help initiate this rich historical sweep will be Sidney H. Griffith's *The Church in the Shadow of the Mosque: Christians and Muslims in the World of Islam* (Princeton, NJ: Princeton University Press, 2008). Griffiths synthesizes years of painstaking scholarship to offer stunning detail regarding the ways the advent of Muslims in the Levant incited fresh initiatives regarding the telling questions of faith in which all of the churches had been so assiduously engaged, often leaving them at odds with one another. It is my contention that a similar opportunity attends us now.

My next mentor was Georges Anawati, OP, a Dominican confrere of Marcel Dubois whose *Introduction à la thélogie musulmane* (Paris: J. Vrin, 1946), composed jointly with Louis Gardet, offers a model for this inquiry undertaken nearly three-quarters of a century later. So I undertake it in grateful recognition of the guidance of these two French Dominicans, hoping to bring to it some of the astuteness of their intellects, as well as the simplicity of their spirit. Moreover, my own experience of comparative inquiry has ever illustrated the wisdom of the American philosopher, Charles Sanders Peirce, reminding us how inextricably triadic is all human apprehension, which I have found to be true of interfaith exchange as well, where dyadic conversation can easily lead to impasses that a third inter-locutor may well unscramble. So while it may appear daunting to expound three traditions rather than two, that very exercise can also facilitate the comparative task, with one or another tradition playing the mediating role as we proceed.

The chronological emergence of the revelations which shape each of these traditions leads ineluctably to later ones presenting them-selves as succeeding – indeed, even superseding – the earlier. Indeed, this dynamic is often inscribed in the founding documents themselves. The way Christians characterize their book as the *New* Testament, while assigning Hebrew Scriptures as the *Old* Testament, offers a classical paradigm of this maneuver. Muslim tradition presents the Qur'an as culminating the revelations to Moses and in Jesus, yet the book itself does one better by insisting that it initiates believers into the originary "religion of Abraham" (3:95). Here supersession meets the original to offer a complete package. Yet Christians make similar claims in presenting their revelation as "the Word who made the universe," now become human in Jesus, so eternally finessing all claims to historical pre-eminence. Without pretending to set aside this chronological pattern, this inquiry will proceed more diachronically to show how each tradition, as it develops, displays features cognate to the other, usually with little actual contact. In that sense, we may call this an exercise in "creative hermeneutics," detailing what we are able to discern in retrospect in a completely different interfaith milieu.

Our strategy will indirectly corroborate the (sometime contested) fact that Jews, Christians, and Muslim do worship the same God. Christians who might doubt this could easily find Christian Arabs directing their eucharistic prayer to Allah, yet our approach will address the question in time-honored philosophical fashion, while respecting the fact that our God ever remains unknown. That is the simple observation that if it walks like a duck, quacks like a duck, and tastes like a duck, it is a duck! So each tradition will privilege certain scriptural texts, which coalesce to offer a portrait of the God they worship in a catalog of "names" or "attributes." From that initial platform, we shall observe how each of these traditions elaborates its original revelation, struggling to articulate features of the relations between the freely creating God and creatures, cumulatively displaying each to be wrestling with features leading to one God.

Indeed, the form of the struggle in one tradition will often mirror that of the other, and in the paradigmatic case of free creation of the universe, we find them actually beholden to one another to elaborate this central teaching. By juxtaposing classical theological themes, we will see how they inevitably emerge in each tradition, as it seeks to articulate dimensions of its revelation which can only leave questions to be pondered. That is indeed the way each will develop a "theology," that is to say, an intellectual inquiry into the givens of faith, which Augustine formulated as "faith seeking understanding." Those dimensions of faith become classical *loci* (or domains) where such questions emerge, identified here as free creation, divine and human freedom, human initiative and trust in divine providence, with the culminating judgment as "consummation," "second coming," or "return." Separate chapters will explore each *locus* comparatively, to note how we can learn about ourselves from each other.

I have suggested calling this inquiry an exercise in "creative hermeneutics," whereby conceptual patterns, often developed separately, can illuminate one another once we see them as executing cognate explorations. This approach reflects the fresh face of interfaith inquiry often associated with the liberating document of Vatican Council II, *Nostra Aetate*, yet more pertinently part of the air we have come to breathe. The Bavarian Catholic theologian, Karl Rahner, attempted to articulate this spirit in an article, entitled

"Towards a Fundamental Interpretation of Vatican II" (1979), where "fundamental" in Germanic parlance tends to mean "what has always already been going on."[2] This seminal lecture at Boston College focused on a Christianity now facing other major religions, much as Jewish Christians of the first century had been faced with pagans wishing to affirm Jesus. That comparison allowed him to offer 70 and 1970 CE as symbolic dates, so bracketing 19 centuries of Western European Christianity (including the missionary movement) to help us recognize how we now stand on the threshold of a "world-church."

The parallels between 70 and 1970 were striking to me at the time, involved as we were in Jewish–Christian understanding, yet become even more so today, as Islam has come to take its place as the inevitable "third" among the Abrahamic faiths. Rahner's precise point is that revelational communities are sometimes called upon to make decisions regarding matters for which the community itself has not yet been able to muster categories sufficient to offer reasons to guide those decisions. In short, they have to "wing it." The example he gives illustrates the emergence of a community of Jewish and Gentile believers in Jesus distinct from what was to become "Judaism," itself a reaction to the new community's formation. Paul trenchantly articulates the conundrum: should pagans who respond to the invitation to follow Jesus first be circumcised to initiate them properly into this community of largely Jewish believers in Jesus? One could certainly have argued that "ontogeny recapitulates phylogeny," so the practice of circumcision could have served as a fitting catechesis, showing how one cannot even speak of Jesus without invoking the entire context of the Scriptures he treasured, with his community, and which he had brought to an incisive focus. Yet Paul insisted on a clean break: no need for them to be circumcised, yet was able to give a rationale, so this landmark decision helped to cinch the "parting of the ways."

In 1979 Rahner could only remind us how underdeveloped was Christian theology to negotiate interfaith issues.[3] Beyond a few intrepid pioneers, like Jules Isaac for Judaism, Louis Massignon for Islam, and Jules Monchanin for Hinduism, there had been little sustained consideration of "other faiths" as a theological issue, thereby reinforcing his selection of 1970 as a symbolic date inaugurating such inquiry. Five years after the Council had ended, we could then begin to see what novel steps *Nostra Aetate* had initiated, making it a landmark document from Vatican II, sharing with *Dignitatis Humanae* the distinction of being the only two which really broke new ground, the rest of the documents having largely disseminated the *nouvelle théologie* to a wider church. In fact, the argument of this very essay would not have been invited or entertained until quite recently. Yet the way it is developed here relies crucially on another Catholic theologian, the Canadian, Bernard Lonergan, whose sense for the intellectual developments latent in a revelational tradition have set the tone for our treatment. His manner of displaying theological inquiry as "faith seeking understanding" will provide us with tools to carry out Rahner's impetus to theological renewal from "other faiths."

Often identified as "a theologian's theologian," Lonergan devoted himself before, during and after Vatican Council II to shaping a mode of thinking which could bring the *ressourcement* elaborated by the *nouvelle théologie* to a systematic focus, thereby showing us how theological attitudes disseminated in that Council might bear fruit in genuine developments in theology. Yet given the relentlessly philosophical quality of the inquiry he stimulated, his "influence" was inevitably more subterranean than evident. All of this should help show how "comparative theology" can contribute to genuine development in Christian theology itself, due perhaps to the staunchly philosophical strategies it must employ to bridge between apparently fixed traditions: showing how they have always been fluid, so that fixing them will betray them as traditions. We can only hope that the same will prove true of Jewish and Muslim readers, as they endeavor to appropriate this exercise in "creative hermeneutics" in ways consonant with their traditions.

The Epilog must contend with a recurring discordant note: each of these traditions has also proved itself to be consonant with the use of force to achieve their ends, in the modern world allowing their cachet to be exploited by political – usually nationalist – leaders to their own ends. How can we explain this? And even more, how can those of us associated with one or another of these traditions employ resources from that same tradition to show how allowing a revelation to be harnessed to the service of power always betrays the tradition itself? Yet each tradition will need first to repent of its collusion with power, before seeking resources to correct what remains an Achilles heel of religion in the modern world. Without the first, we cannot be respected; without attending to the second, we cannot respect ourselves.

Notes

1 For Jewish testimony to the partial rightness of the statement let me cite Jon Levenson arguing with Paul's contention "that one becomes an Israelite through faith into the promise rather than through birth." Levenson insists that "this is not the position of the Hebrew Bible, and it is light years away from the theology of covenant in the Pentateuch. A more accurate statement would be that those who stand under covenantal obligation by nature and necessity are continually called upon to adopt that relationship by free decision. Chosen for service, they must choose to serve." (*Creation and the Persistence of Evil* (San Francisco: Harper & Row, 1987; Princeton, NJ: Princeton University Press, 1994) p. 148). So while being Jewish *ipso facto* implies "covenantal obligation," the manner of fulfilling it invites one to a posture of faith.

2 *Theological Studies* 40 (1979) 716–727.

3 Although Jewish–Christian exchange had begun soon after the publication of *Nostra Aetate* in 1965, a gathering of Jews, Christians, and Muslims at the Tantur Ecumenical Institute in Jerusalem (in 1975), under the inspiration of Sister Marie Goldstein, RSHM, was quite unprecedented in the West. As John Esposito has testified, it would take another ten years for Islam to be recognized as even a potential third partner.

Acknowledgments

As the Preface details, a lasting gift of gratitude comes from my friend of more than half a century, Nikos Stavroulakis, now animator of the Etz Hayyim synagogue in Hania in Crete (www.etz-hayyim-hania.org/), to whose graciousness this work is dedicated on behalf of those who have experienced it.

More immediate thanks to Paul Murray and to Tony Currer of Durham, whose roles in both the Alan Richardson and Cuthbert fellowships gave me the freedom and daily inspiration to execute this task. A special gratitude to Paul Murray and the electors of the Richardson fellowship for extending it to me for the Michaelmas term 2009, which provided access to sterling colleagues in the Faculty of Theology of Durham University, with the time and space to complete this study. And to the choral and ministry staff of Durham Cathedral, who provided a reflective evensong to cap my daily efforts. The rhythm sustaining each day was supplied by Father Currer and our student complement at St Cuthbert's parish house: Benedict Douglas, Tommy Humphries, and Patricia Kelly, who united to begin each day with morning prayer and extended to our supper together, prepared by the one determined at breakfast. A splendid community of work and prayer, which spiced the term immeasurably, gracefully facilitated by Helen Lawless, valiant administrative assistant of St Cuthbert's parish.

Finally, to Lewis Ayres, Bede Professor at Durham (the series editor who accepted this second book for Blackwell), and to Rebecca Harkin, faithful Blackwell editor to so many over the years, as well as her valiant assistants: Bridget Jennings, Sally Cooper, and most recently, Isobel Bainton, for seeing the manuscript through to a meticulous finish, a task every author especially appreciates.

Credits

Chapter 4. Jean-Pierre de Caussade: One abandoning oneself to divine providence. Excerpts from pp. 27–28, 31, 34, 51, 72–74, 87, 90, 102–3 from *The Sacrament of the Present Moment by Jean-Pierre de Caussade*. English translation copyright © 1981 by William Collins Sons & Co. Ltd. Introduction © 1982 by Harper & Row, Publishers, Inc. Reprinted by permission of HarperCollins Publishers.

Chapter 5. The point of it all: "return," judgment, and "second coming"; creation to consummation. Excerpts from pp. 526, 554, 560, 562 and 670 from Sadr al-Din al-Shirazi [Mulla Sadra] *The Divine Manifestations of the Secrets of the Perfecting Sciences*, translated and annotated Fazel Asadi Amjad, Mahdi Dasht Bozorgi reprinted by permission of ICAS Press.

Every effort has been made to trace copyright holders and to obtain their permission for the use of copyright material. The publisher apologizes for any errors or omissions in the above list and would be grateful if notified of any corrections that should be incorporated in future reprints or editions of this book.

Introduction

Modes of Comparing: Doctrines as Precipitation of Practices

Comparing religious traditions demands that we attend to the pluriform structure of their practices. For attentiveness of that sort will alert us to the inherently analogous character of any assertions which might be made. Here George Lindbeck's invitation to regard doctrine as precipitations or distillations of practices makes eminent sense. Or Bernard Lonergan's strategy for properly understanding assertions a tradition might make, as in pronouncements of early church councils: "if these are to be regarded as answers, we must first grasp the questions which they are proposed to answer," questions arising as believers seek to relate religious practices to the milieu in which they live. So Jews and early Christians were readily accused of idolatry in the Roman Empire, in the face of their resistance to state deities; the defense would reveal how their beliefs structured their lives, as their mode of life would clarify

Towards a Jewish-Christian-Muslim Theology, First Edition. David B. Burrell.
© 2011 John Wiley & Sons Ltd. Published 2011 by John Wiley & Sons Ltd.

those beliefs. In short, "doctrines" prove to be secondary in the life of believers, though they answer the need for clarity in the face of challenge. None of this would be news to practitioners of these traditions, which offers a far better descriptor than "believer." For while adhering to certain beliefs is also a practice, everything depends on the way one adheres to them, which will best be revealed in practices collateral to assertions. To borrow a striking example from George Lindbeck, a crusader invoking God in striking down Muslim believers says a great deal more about his belief-structure, and indeed about his god, than could ever be told from his reciting the creed. So an account which tries to compare different traditions must always subject itself to personal experience, to artistic re-enactments, as well as alternative scenarios, for such is the pluriform richness of religious tradition.

How Historical Positioning of Traditions Invites "Supersessionist" Strategies to Understand the Earlier

The three traditions grouped under "Abrahamic faiths" have a special difficulty relating to each other, given the unalterable order of their chronological appearance. Indeed, given their close association, it would be surprising if the successor tradition did not consider itself to be superior to, or even claim to replace its predecessor, as we have already noted. Moreover, the propensity to consider what comes later to be better may be even more ingrained than Hegel's legacy, for successor traditions will spontaneously argue their superiority from a chronological appeal. Yet Foucault's strategy of intellectual "archaeology" will offer the antidote needed to restore this imbalance, reminding us how easily we will fail to construe a succeeding generation if we neglect to identify the lineaments of predecessors in its very structure. Paul encapsulates this reality when he insists, to the pagans of Rome becomes Christians, that "you, a wild olive shoot, were grafted in [the

Jews'] place to share in the richness of the olive tree" (Rom. 11:17). His insistence received spontaneous testimony in a 1975 visit to Mbarara to celebrate 75 years of Catholic Christianity in Uganda. Stunned at how recent this had been, I turned to some "White Fathers" (Missionary Society of Africa), asking them how their community had portrayed the initial contact. For they could hardly say: "I want to tell you about Jesus," lacking any effective context for such an introduction. The response was telling. As they had gleaned it, pioneers in this endeavor listened to the people's stories, responding with "we have stories like that: there was this man Abraham ... ," thereby corroborating Paul's point as well as receiving good marks as missionaries: they learned the language and they listened! Indeed, had succeeding Christian communities continued to introduce Jesus in that way Christians would not find it surprising that Jesus, Mary, and Joseph were Jews.

Yet a Western mentality finds it all too easy to overlook the past, especially in the interests of bolstering a successor's pre-eminence. So this inquiry will introduce ways of countering that propensity, much as interfaith friendships do in individual lives, by focusing on practices which bring traditions into effective contact with one another: times, postures, rhythms of prayer; as well as patterns for appropriating revelation to meet contemporary challenges. The last century evidenced how easily ignorance of the ways one tradition is rooted in its predecessor can lead to denigrating and even despising individuals who exemplify an earlier tradition. The roots of this propensity, however, can be traced to a modern fascination with progress which fueled colonization as well, often soliciting religious sanctions to eradicate signs of a purportedly backward ethos. Yet as we come to realize the negative side of modernism, from colonization to ecological depredation, successor traditions can be helped to a more positive appreciation of their predecessors. Indeed, those of us who enjoy live interfaith contacts discover our own shortcomings by appropriating what we learn from those of other faiths about the God we share.

Practices as Practical Bridges: Times, Postures, Rhythms of Prayer; Patterns of Appropriation

Yet how can Abrahamic believers be said to share one God, when much of the interaction, and even their revelational deliverances, are polemical in character, sometimes explicitly directed against "the other?" Crafting a proper response to this vexing question has shaped the approach of this inquiry, urging us to begin with practices, in the light of which we will be better equipped to parse contentious statements. Jewish–Christian interaction offers a telling example. It is easy to oppose the two traditions starkly: Christians believe Jesus is the "Son of God" while Jews regard him yet another pretender; no way to cross that chasm! Yet when we participate as two communities at prayer, only to realize that Christians have never found a better communal prayer than the psalms, we find ourselves side-by-side praying to one God: the giver of the covenant to Moses, whom Christians have come to recognize as the father of Jesus as well. And when monks observe Muslims praying five times daily, accompanied by a haunting call to prayer and deep bodily obeisance, they are palpably reminded of their form of life canonized by Benedict. And Syriac Christians can even detect vestiges of their own chant in the call to prayer. For someone whose approach to religious traditions is primarily conceptual or doctrinal, these may appear to be accidental appurtenances, yet it is such rhythms of prayer which decisively form believers into the contours of their faith, as Shabbat does Jews, eucharistic celebration does Catholics, and polyphonic hymnody, Mennonites; and daily prayers and seasonal fasting (with pilgrimage) does Muslims.

Correlative to communal worship are ways each tradition appropriates its revelation into daily life, where marked differences also betray similar patterns. As Muslim children are offered stories of Muhammad to guide them to proper reactions to a playground bully, Christian children will be instructed by the evangelical charter of Matthew 25 to share what they have with less fortunate children when the opportunity emerges, and Jewish children to respect the elders of their community, who pass on to them precious traditions delineating their special, God-given, identity. The thrust of this early formation reminds them that theirs is a communal commitment which reaches into daily life, inevitably reflected in their relations with an encompassing society. It is here that most of us come to discern the shape of other faith communities, to discover where we diverge or converge in characteristic attitudes. The Muslim world, for example, is studded with primary and secondary schools animated by Catholic religious communities, where the practices embedded in those institutions convey more about Catholic Christianity then any set of teachings. They also dramatize a salient difference within Christianity, as well, for Catholics feel little compulsion to proselytize, confident that the charter of Matthew 25 is sufficiently evident in the organization of their studies as well as in extra-curricular activities of service. Needless to say, this makes them especially welcomed in the Islamic world.

Using Philosophical Tools that Unravel "Doctrinal Disputes"; "Intellectual Therapy" (Wittgenstein)

Following the trail of practices, let us not forget that elaborating a tradition intellectually represents a practice as well. At this point, each tradition found itself having recourse to philosophical strategies to help unravel *aporiae* (or persistent conundrums) left by their respective revelations. What will prove remarkable, as we trace the strategies employed to illuminate each theme, are traits common to the intellectual therapies undertaken. For philosophy exhibits its usefulness more in mediating disputes lingering from oppositions (or even contradictions) latent in revelational texts, than it does in attempting to "explain" them "systematically." I hope to show that this manner of articulating the role philosophical strategies play in elaborating traditions, borrowed from Wittgenstein, more accurately limns their fruitfulness than any "systematic" pretensions. His approach will also display how the medieval trope of "handmaid" dignifies philosophy's role in these arenas rather than denigrating it. For pretending to a magisterial role *in divinis* (matters concerning God) can only augur pretention.

Dialog and Proclamation: Assessing the Truth of a Tradition

A final caveat concerning a purported opposition between *dialog* and *proclamation*. Dialog, like any probing conversation, attends to *meaning* rather than *truth*. This should be evident enough, but attempts to contrast "dialog" starkly with "proclamation" have obscured this simple point, by implying that dialog is radically deficient as a faith-strategy, since it stops short of proclaiming the truth. But what would it be to proclaim the truth? Would it be to make an assertion and then to insist that it was true; or as one wag put it: to stamp one's foot? In fact, any properly formed assertion, actually stated, intends what is the case. Grammar is inherently ethical, so lying – deliberately stating what is not the case – is inherently wrong. Yet we know that our acceptance of what another says is often conditioned by the moral probity or veracity of the speaker. So "proclaiming the truth" of one's faith is better done than said, as the Amish community in Pennsylvania demonstrated to America by forgiving their children's killer. Merely stating one's faith convictions cannot in fact count as proclamation. What counts is witness; and while the fact of dialog may give telling witness in certain situations, like Israel/Palestine, the intellectual endeavor of dialog can at best be a means of sorting out awkward from promising ways of stating what we believe. Yet this is hardly a deficiency; it is simply what any conversation tries to do. Authentic proclamation is quite another thing, as the Gospels remind us again and again.

John Henry Newman, Bernard Lonergan, and Nicholas Lash can each be invoked as witnesses to this crucial distinction. Newman reminds us (in *Grammar of Assent*) how sinuous is the path to arriving at truth, and how delicate are the balancing judgments involved.[1] Bernard Lonergan directly acknowledges Newman's reflections when he parses Aquinas's insistence that truth can only be ascertained by way of judgment.[2] And Nicholas Lash's *Theology for Pilgrims* deftly exhibits the quality of dialectical reasoning which must attend reliable judgment.[3] In the spirit of Wittgenstein, the witness Lash's writing gives to constructive and critical dialog offers a healthy antidote to television confrontations which leave listeners to "make up their own minds." One can almost hear Wittgenstein query: "I know how to make up my bed, but how might I make up my mind?" So whatever effective proclamation might be, it cannot be had without probing discussion and the conceptual clarification that dialog can bring. Reduced to forthright assertion or downright insistence, it can neither be authentic nor effective. So there is no substitute for attending to meanings, as we attempt to minimize infelicitous expression in matters "pertaining to God and the things of God" (as Aquinas views theology). For the same thinker reminds us that our language *at best* can but "imperfectly signify God" (*Summa Theologiae* 1.13.3). In that vein, this inquiry will not attempt to assess which (if any) of these traditions is *true*, but it should assist believers in each to find their way to assessing – as best they can, and must – the truth of their tradition. Yet we should also appreciate how this can be a lifelong project.

Notes

1 Consult preferably Nicholas Lash's edition of Newman's *An Essay in Aid of a Grammar of Assent* (Notre Dame, IN: University of Notre Dame Press, 1979) for its illuminating introduction.

2 Bernard Lonergan, *Verbum: Word and Idea in Aquinas* (eds Frederick E. Crowe, and Robert M. Doran; Toronto: University of Toronto Press, 1996).

3 Nicholas Lash, *Theology for Pilgrims* (Notre Dame, IN: University of Notre Dame Press, 2008).

1

Free Creation as a Shared Task for Jews, Christians, Muslims[1]

It is certainly remarkable that it took the fledgling Christian movement four centuries to respond to its central faith question concerning Jesus: who and what is he? Moreover, the long-standing quest
for clarity regarding Jesus doubtless overshadowed more explicit
reflection on the first article of the creed as well: "I believe in God,
the Father almighty, creator of heaven and earth". As Robert
Sokolowski observes: "The issue the church had to settle first, once
it acquired public and official recognition under Constantine and
could turn to controversies regarding its teaching, was the issue of
the being and actions of Christ." Yet he goes on to insist:

> [While] the Council of Chalcedon, and the councils and controversies
> that led up to it, were concerned with the mystery of Christ ... they
> also tell us about the God who became incarnate in Christ. They tell
> us first that God does not destroy the natural necessities of things he
> becomes involved with, even in the intimate union of the incarnation.
> What is according to nature, and what reason can disclose in nature,

---

Towards a Jewish-Christian-Muslim Theology, First Edition. David B. Burrell.
© 2011 John Wiley & Sons Ltd. Published 2011 by John Wiley & Sons Ltd.

retains it integrity before the Christian God [who] is not a part of the world and is not a "kind" of being at all. Therefore, the incarnation is not meaningless or impossible or destructive.[2]

Moreover, what Sokolowski calls

the Christian distinction between God and the world, the denial that God in his divinity is part of or dependent on the world, was brought forward with greater clarity through the discussion of the way the Word became flesh. The same distinction was also emphasized as a background for the Trinitarian doctrines and for the controversies about grace ... Thus many of the crucial dogmatic issues raised in the relationship between God and the world, and the positions judged to be erroneous would generally have obscured the Christian distinction between the divine and the mundane.[3]

So creation not only comes first, as it were, in our God's transactions with the world; it is also true that the way we understand that founding relation will affect our attempts to articulate any further interaction. For were the One who reached out to believers "in Christ" not the creator of heaven and earth, the story would have to be told in a vastly different (and inescapably mythic) idiom, as indeed it has often been on the part of Christians so preoccupied with redemption that creation is simply presumed as its stage-setting.

And understandably enough, since the narrative of incarnation and redemption captures the lion's share of the tripartite creed associated with the initiation rites of baptism, creation can appear as a mere preamble. Moreover, an adequate treatment of the unique activity which constitutes creating, as well as the quite ineffable relation between creatures and creator which it initiates, will tax one's philosophical resources to the limit, so more timid theologians (with philosophers of religion) prefer to finesse it altogether. Yet as Sokolowski reminds us, we cannot afford to do that since the interaction among these shaping mysteries of faith is at once palpable and mutually illuminating. Nor can Christians treat Hebrew Scriptures as a mere preamble to their revelation of God in Jesus, since the God whom Jesus can call "Abba" is introduced in those very Scriptures. Moreover, the Hebrew Scriptures reflect similar structural parallels between *creation* and *redemption*, as the engaging story of God's affair with Israel begins at Genesis 12 with Abraham, while the initial chapters detailing God's creation of the universe seem designed to offer a universal grounding to that story.

By the time medieval thinkers came to engage these issues, however, a third Abrahamic voice clamored for recognition, reflecting a fresh scripture. The Qur'an's account is far more lapidary: "He says 'be' and it is" (6:73), yet the pattern is repeated. The heart of the drama turns on Muhammad's God-given "recitation"; while Allah's identifying Himself with "the Creator of the heavens and the earth" (2:117) assures us that we are not merely trafficking with an Arabian deity. So the forces conspiring to elaborate a Christian "doctrine of creation" were at once historical and conceptual, scriptural and philosophical, with parallel discussions in other faiths shaping the context.[4] Both Jewish and Christian readings of Genesis approached the equivocal language regarding pre-existent stuff as part of the inherently narrative structure of the work, insisting that God created the universe *ex nihilo*; that is, without presupposing anything "to work on." So the philosophical task will be to articulate how such "sheer origination" could even be possible, while the theological goal will be to show the action to be utterly gratuitous. For if creator and creation are to be what the Hebrew Scriptures presume them to be, neither stuff nor motive can be presupposed. Here is where what Sokolowski identifies as "the distinction" proves so critical: creation can only be creation if God can be God without creating. No external incentive nor internal need can induce God to create, for this creator need not create to be the One by whom all that is can originate. Yet if creating adds nothing to God, who gains nothing by creating, what could such a One be, and how might we characterize that One?

So the way we treat the act originating the universe will lead us inexorably to the One originating it, as whatever we can say about that One will shape our way of considering the One's activity. So creation is not only first chronologically, as it were, but first

11

conceptually as well. Yet there are bound to have been alternative accounts, since the question of origination arises naturally for us, evidenced in countless stories offering to articulate the process. As the move to more methodical considerations of these issues gained momentum in Greece, however, questions about origins were eclipsed by considerations of the structure of the universe. As Plato's *Timaeus* proceeds mythologically at crucial junctures, Aristotle could deftly avoid the origins question. Yet by the time our respective religious traditions turned their attention to God as creator, a powerful philosophical figure had emerged from the Hellenic matrix: Plotinus. His relentlessly logical mind traced a multifarious universe to one principle, as the necessary condition for the order inherent in it, extending Plato's pregnant image of *participation* yet further to speak of the manner by which the ordered universe originates as *emanating* from the One. As with Plato before him, Plotinus had recourse to metaphor to signal the limits to conceptual inquiry. Yet as we have just suggested, the *manner* will offer the only clue we can have to the character of the One originating. So as we shall see, Plotinus's interpretation founders precisely on whether that "coming forth" is best described in terms of logical deduction, or whether it results from a free act of the One. At this point the deliverances of revelation and what was taken to be reason initially clashed, though further inquiry by illustrious thinkers would find them complementing one another.

Yet as circumstance would have it, creation offers the one area where we can track interaction of some kind among these three traditions.[5] The interaction we can trace occurred as each tradition sought to clarify scriptural accounts of the origin of the universe – identical for Jews and Christians, and substantially the same for Muslims. Much work has been done to situate the Genesis story in the context of origin stories from the milieu in which the Hebrew Scriptures emanate, noting how the scriptural account reflects that milieu, and how it differs. Genesis shows traces of earlier accounts in postulating a chaotic matrix in need of ordering; but contrasts starkly in the manner of achieving that order. Earlier origin accounts graphically depict struggle, issuing in dismembering and reconstituting, while

Genesis focuses on crafting or even more refined: executing by verbal command. However, we might conceive the pre-existent matrix, which remains utterly obscure, it offers no resistance to being ordered, so the divine act of originating and of ordering remains sovereign. That could be one reason why the matrix dropped from sight, reduced to a shadowy "prime matter" in Hellenic philosophical accounts, and to *nothing* in religious accounts. Yet the official *nothing* will return to undermine religious accounts in the form of primordial resistance to the sovereign action of God, dramatized in spiritual creatures as *sin*. Jon Levenson offers a remarkable delineation of this inescapable dimension of the Jewish tradition in his aptly titled *Creation and the Persistence of Evil,* contrasting it sharply with what emerged in all three traditions as creation *ex nihilo*.[6] Yet in response to the Preface to the second (1994) edition of this work, I shall propose an understanding of creation *ex nihilo* whereby the opposition need not be so stark.

So it may well be that Plotinus's magisterial account of emanation from the One proved less useful to a religious articulation of origins precisely because it was so magisterial, leaving too little room for any palpable resistance to an account of divine creating, relegating that feature to a *matter* residual to the outpouring of being as it transmutes into becoming. Yet once the influential Islamic philosopher, al-Farabi, introduced the model of logical deduction to provide a firm structure to Plotinus's metaphor of overflowing, the model itself implied necessity, so settling the ambiguity remaining from Plotinus: does this emanation from the One take place necessarily, as a consequence of its nature, or as an intentional free act? In the end, however, the very feature which made the logical model attractive to philosophers made it repugnant to religious thinkers, intent on accentuating divine freedom in creating. The potential of freedom to be read as arbitrary led philosophers away from it, while religious thinkers found a necessary emanation to compromise the divine One by demanding that God could not be God without creating the universe. Yet by the same reasoning, would not the logical model also effectively adulterate Plotinus's One, by endowing it with the necessary attribute of creator?

So we can recognize tensions which could arise between philosophical strategies and religious sensibilities, made all the more inevitable since thinking believers could hardly dispense with the tools of human reason to articulate the path revealed to lead them to truth. Yet while each of the Abrahamic traditions sought ways to negotiate this tension, in the case of creation they received help from one another, albeit in sequential fashion. This actual interaction privileges *creation* for comparative purposes, of course, and serendipitously so, since we will see how every other topic will return to the way one attempts to articulate the ineffable relation between creatures and creator. Moreover, the period fruitful for comparing ways of treating creation – from al-Ghazali (d. 1111) to Aquinas (d. 1274) – enjoyed a relatively homogeneous philosophical culture as well, so adherents of diverse religious traditions were able to share a common discourse. Avicenna had transmitted Aristotle to each principal: Ghazali, Moses ben Maimon (Maimonides), and Thomas Aquinas; so much so that Maimonides will often identify Avicenna's views with Aristotle. None of them actually met the other, but those who came later were able to profit from earlier thinkers, in some cases actually citing them in critical conversation, often showing their esteem for the other by taking issue with them, as philosophers are wont to do. So Ghazali, who is trenchantly critical of some of Avicenna's conclusions regarding points of faith, will also acknowledge his philosophical debt by structuring his natural philosophy along Avicennian lines.[7] But the sticking point remains whether creation constitutes the initial moment in time, or whether (as the necessary emanation scheme proposed) the universe had no beginning, so that creatures were coeternal with their creating principle. Ghazali tends to link an initial moment of the universe with creation as a free and intentional activity. As if to display his dependence on Ghazali (which most presume to be the case), Maimonides inherited this criterion, insisting that an everlasting creation coterminous with the creator itself could not be free but would inescapably reflect necessary emanation. Furthermore, nothing seemed to divide "philosophers" from "theologians" so much as the contention that the universe would have to have had a beginning if it were truly to be created. Necessary emanation might be proffered as a theory of origination, but never as a way of explicating the statements of the Bible or Qur'an about God's free act of creating.

Yet this very contention would be challenged by Thomas Aquinas, a thinker "in conversation with" both Avicenna and to Maimonides, though far less acquainted with the work of Ghazali. (He was "in conversation" in the sense that we are always contending with writers who impress us, allowing their mode of inquiry to affect our own, to learn from them in the process. Indeed, we have to acknowledge this to be a singularly fruitful way of meeting others without ever having personal contact with them.) Aquinas adopted Avicenna's axial distinction of *essence* from *existing*, though radically recasting it, to adapt the metaphysics he gleaned from Aristotle (often through Avicenna's commentary) to accommodate a universe freely created by one God. Yet so Herculean a task, while reflective of Aquinas's singular genius, could hardly have been executed without Avicenna's quite Islamic innovation on Aristotle's treatment, later confirmed in the central role Maimonides gives to existence, as it is conveyed to creatures from a God who possesses it necessarily – Avicenna's way of establishing "the distinction" between creator and creatures.

Yet Aquinas would see that, once such a "distinction" had been secured, it mattered little whether creation was conceived with or without a beginning. He also profited from Maimonides' clearheaded observation that since neither position could be demonstrated, Torah-believers were free to accept the language of Genesis, which implied an initial moment, at face value. Yet while he averred what revelation stated to be the case, Aquinas argued that a creation coterminous with the creator need not derogate from the primary asseveration of each tradition about creating: that the act must be free and intentional. In other words, while insisting on free creation, the primary focus of revelation is not so much on an initial moment but on the way each creature depends on the sustaining power of God for its very existence at every moment. That is the radical revision of Aristotle which the Bible effects: asserting that what Aristotle took to be the lynchpin of his metaphysics – substance, existing in

15

itself – rather exists by the power of a creator sustaining it in existence. The verses of the Qur'an or of Genesis 1–3, of course, hardly succeed in making that point, yet a concerted inquiry carried out by Muslim, Jewish, and Christian "interlocutors" (in the sense proposed) did reach that formidable conclusion, and in doing so illustrates how revelation can so illuminate the strategies of philosophy as to transform them. For our three signal Abrahamic thinkers – Ghazali, Maimonides, and Aquinas – each adopt a dialectical approach to persuade their fellow believers how fruitfully reason and faith can interact with each other. And one of them, Aquinas, coming last as he did, was able to utilize the others to illuminate his work, with a dialectical strategy which allows faith and reason mutually to illuminate one another.

Islamic reflection treated this subject in a sustained philosophical manner before the other traditions, profiting from Syriac translators rendering Hellenic philosophical texts into Arabic. But their primary source remains the Qur'an: "Originator (*Badî'*) of the heavens and earth. When He decrees a thing, He says only 'Be!' And it is" (Qur'an 2:117). There are eight names for God, among the canonical 99, which direct our attention to Allah as the source of all that is: *al-Badî'* (Absolute Cause), *al-Bâri'* (Producer), *al-Khâliq* (Creator), *al-Mubdi'* (Beginner), *al-Muqtadir* (All-Determiner), *al-Musawwir* (Fashioner), *al-Qâdir* (All-Powerful), *al-Qahhâr* (Dominator), each with various connotations of creating.[8] Indeed, nothing seems simpler than identifying the one God as creator of all that is. Yet if the God of Abraham can be defined, as Thomas Aquinas does at the outset of his *Summa Theologiae*, as "the beginning and end of all things, and especially of rational creatures," that lapidary formula has but one clear implication: God is not one of those things, an affirmation which sums up Islamic *tawhîd*.[9] For confessing divine unity (*tawhîd*) entails removing all so-called "gods" from the world; indeed, replacing them all with One whose originating relation to the universe offers enduring testimony to the utter uniqueness of the attestation: "there is no God but God," novel and intractable as it is in human discourse. Yet while this affirmation may prove congruent to human reason, by contrast to a mythological proliferation of gods, it will also prove to be its stumbling block, implicitly testifying how its corollary, creation, must properly be rooted in revelation.

There will be no one Muslim account of creation; indeed there can be no fully adequate account, so the plurality of accounts is less a sign of the inadequacy of Muslim thinkers to their task than it is of their fidelity to the founding revelation of their tradition: to *tawhîd* and its corollary, creation. Irony reigns here: any pretension to have articulated the founding relation adequately will have reduced that relation to one comprehensible to us, so undermining and nullifying the distinction expressed by *tawhîd*, the heart of this tradition. The stumbling block which *tawhîd* becomes as one tries to render it conceptually may be identified by these incisive queries: everything which is not God comes forth from God yet cannot exist without God, so how are they distinct when they cannot be sepa-rated? If God is eternal and everything else temporal, how does the act of creating bridge that chasm? If God alone properly exists, and everything else exists by an existence derived from divine existence, how *real* are the things we know? And the clincher: if God makes everything else to be, including human actions, how can our actions be properly our own? That is, how can we be responsible for what God makes to be? How can God's actions, in other words, be imputed to us? And if they cannot, to what end is the Qur'an a warning and a guide? This last conundrum proved to be the crux, as we shall see later. For now, it is enough to note how what seems so simple – identifying the one God as creator of all that is – will introduce us into the set of intractable issues we call theology.

So questions elicited by the straightforward insistence that "God says 'be!' and it is" will require all the philosophical sophistication one can muster, yet two distinct schools emerge in Islamic thought: *kalâm* ("theology") and *falsafa* ("philosophy"). Notable exceptions to this apparent polarization in the Sunni world were al-Ghazâlî (d. 1111) and Fakhr al-Din al-Râzî (d. 1209), who prove to be as familiar with the thought of Islamic "philosophers" as with reli-gious thinkers. Our treatment will attend to the points where concerns intersect, and where recognizable tendencies display complementary aspects of the relation between a creator God and creation itself. Here Ian Netton's formulation of "the Qur'ânic Creator Paradigm," as he puts it, can usefully guide our inquiry by forming the undeniable setting for further conceptual quandaries. It "embraces a God who (1) creates *ex nihilo*; (2) acts definitively in historical time; (3) guides His people in such time; and (4) can in some way be known indirectly by His creation."[10] We must add a fifth feature as well, presumed in the first three: (5) that God's mode of acting be free. It should be clear how many philosophical conundra lurk in each of these assertions: what is it to create? How does an eternal God act in time? How can divine guidance be carried out and received? What are the ways in which created things can entice a created intellect to some knowledge of their divine source? What sense can we have of the sovereign freedom of God in creating, of creation's utter gratuity? Once having identified the usual groupings of Islamic thinkers reflecting on such matters – *kalâm*, *falsafa*, and *ishrâq* – we shall have occasion to attend to the way each group will respect the five features of the paradigm as we consider further topics germane to free creation, noting how they function as virtual corollaries to this central teaching.

It is worth reflecting why creation is so critical for Islam. For if all that is emanates from the one God, this must include the "straight path" as it comes down to the Prophet, as well as the "gospel" and the "Torah," which Muslims teach were also given to humankind by God. Moreover, beyond asserting that there is but one God who freely creates the universe, *tawhid* insists that this creator is utterly one. Yet if God is to be utterly simple, the acts of creating and of revealing cannot be separate actions; sending the Qur'an will complete the gratuitous act of creating, already elaborated in the Torah and the Gospel. So proffering the covenant to all humankind completes creation as well:

> And when your Lord took the progeny of the sons of Adam from their loins, He took them to witness on their own souls, saying: "Am I not your Lord?" They answered: "Yes, indeed, we witness to it" – this, lest you should say on the Day of resurrection: "We had not known it to be so" (7:172).[11]

So the Qur'an sees itself expressing the "religion of Abraham" (3:95) in such a way as to embrace all humankind, covenanted to God from the beginning. Indeed, this God's creating humankind will lead seamlessly to a call to respond, as the inbuilt task of a "vice-gerent" of creation will be to recapitulate the originating emanation by returning it to the One from whom it comes. Many will fail to do so, of course, yet the Qur'an, in coming down, proffers all the help one needs to execute that task, so completing creation.

On the Jewish side, free creation serves to corroborate the uncontested primacy of the God who covenants the people Israel, whose destiny and vagaries constitute the dominant narrative of the Hebrew Scriptures. Placing the creation story first in their canonical redaction serves this purpose rather than pretending to offer a cosmological account. Indeed, as Moses Maimonides interprets the Scriptures in terms of the dominant philosophy of his day, he tends to presume the free founding act of origination, to focus on ways we might be able to parse the ensuing relation. He capitalizes on Avicenna's distinction of *existing* from *essence* to insist that in God "essence and existence are perfectly identical" (*Guide* 1.57), to secure the "distinction" of creator from creatures. Yet his radical agnosticism regarding any linkage between them, even when creation itself implies one, will decisively shape the way he explores creatures relating to their creator, to elaborate the salient corollaries of creation which we shall soon be considering: divine sovereignty and human freedom, providence, and the ultimate return of creation to its creator. Yet moving too quickly to Maimonides' philosophical interpretation of the Scriptures could easily elide formidable objections to an uncontested primacy for the God who covenants the people Israel, as Jon Levenson has so ably argued. Moreover, his optic will prove germane to the way all three traditions reflect on free creation, especially in their growing concurrence in creation *ex nihilo*, despite preponderant evidence to the contrary in the Genesis account.

For while the creator whom the Hebrew Scriptures and the Qur'an celebrate acts without a concomitant struggle – "God said 'be' and it is" – there remains an undertone of a resistant matrix which will emerge again and again as the narrative unfolds. Indeed, even the resulting philosophical formulation "ex nihilo" cannot succeed in reducing the primordial chaos literally to *nothing*. For it will remain present as an asystematic factor, dramatized in the trickster figure of Satan, only to emerge in Hellenic dress as *matter*. So summarizing biblical and Qur'anic free creation as "uncontested" can only intend to eliminate any hint of dualism from a creation account, as in classic Manichean pictures. For as Augustine came to see, these prove to be jejune, giving the manifest struggle between *good* and *evil* a metaphysical status. Yet the originary matrix of Genesis can hardly be neatly eliminated in favor of a translucent word, for resistance perdures in one form or another. That is the nub of Jon Levenson's thesis, though its implications may not reach as far as his commentary suggests. His exposition highlights our incapacity to conceptualize creation, as does Paul's recalling that "we know that the whole creation has been groaning in labor pains until now; and not only the creation but we ourselves, who have the first fruits of the Spirit, groan inwardly while we wait for adoption, the redemption of our bodies" (Rom. 8:22). The intractable resistance that we all experience, in the world about us where it meets our own bodies, is an inescapable part of God's creation, challenging any purported account of creation *ex nihilo* which would import a lightsome reading of "God saw that it was good." And those accounts Levenson is right to overturn: "the residue of the static Aristotelian conception of deity as perfect, unchanging being; the uncritical tendency to affirm the constancy of divine action; and the conversion of biblical theology into an affirmation of the goodness of whatever is."[12] Yet as endemic as it is, resistance cannot play the role of a "worthy opponent," for as Augustine also saw: God and goodness can have no competitors, as though *good* or *evil* could represent equal options. For as much as that gnostic picture pretends to articulate the dramatic conflict between good and evil in our world, ironically enough, treating *evil* as anything other than a *privation* neutralizes its peculiar potency: to leave an unwarranted hole in the fabric of God's creation. (Indeed, what arrests us about evil actions, teaching us to call them *evil*, is the disruption they cause, their inherently diremptive character which fractures, as it were, in the texture of reality, arresting us forcibly as it does so.) So while Levenson's insightful reading of the Hebrew Scriptures can duly expose "philosophical" misreadings of the text, his polemical way of dismissing alternatives can distract us from illuminating philosophical attempts to articulate this founding mystery, some of which we shall attend to, chastened by the uncanny resistance to order we feel around us and in ourselves.[13]

The thinker I find most illuminating in this regard, who learned a great deal from Maimonides, is Thomas Aquinas. Early in his life of reflection he had quite transformed Aristotle, recasting Avicenna's primal distinction between *essence* and *existing* by elevating *existing* from the oxymoronic status of an *accident* to that of *act*: *existing* will be a primary exemplar in the created order of acts as we know them, since only existing things can act. This philosophical strategy allowed him to identify a trace of God's creative activity in creatures, as each participates in the gift of existing as it comes forth from the creator, who has been identified as "existing itself" (*ipsum esse*), thereby highlighting what Avicenna and Maimonides had both seen but failed to exploit. Aquinas effectively employed this metaphysical discovery to dismiss any residue of "deity as perfect, unchanging being," with his focus on *act* transcending both stasis and change, as befits a free creator eternally in act. We may then say that the One whose very essence is to exist creates by acting consonant with its nature, though we will be unable to ascertain *how* that might happen, since we cannot properly conceive one whose essence is to exist. Now such "unknowing" must characterize our speech about God who, as creator, cannot properly be an item in the created universe. Yet the uniqueness of the creator/creature relationship will allow Aquinas to use Plotinus's term "emanation" for creating, once having established that God's creating will be freely executed.

It follows from this that it would be improper to try to conceive of the creator as "over against" the created universe, as though it were a separate being, since every creature exists only by *participating* in the inexhaustible act of existing which is the creator. That is, no creature can *be* without its inherent link to the creator, so these

"two" can never be separate from one another, as individual creatures are from each other.

Yet the very act of creation brings about creatures with a life of
their own, so this ineffable "distinction" of creatures from creator
emerges in the act of creating itself. All of this discourse has one
goal: to clarify as best we can the protean expressions of "emanation" and "participation," and do so in such a way that what results
is a gift. So "emanation," "participation," and "gift" form a triptych
expressing the unique act which is creation, bringing about creatures whose very existing consists in their relating to their creator.
So what Aristotle had identified as "existing in itself," individual
subsistent things, are now deemed to exist in relation to a creator.
Yet whatever exists does so in a certain way, for things need to be
identified by their kinds; there is no coherent answer to the query:
how many things are there in the room? Here we are returned to
Aristotle: the puppies born as a result of the coupling of a dog and
a bitch belong to that species, yet the fact of their being born elicits
delight and joy. Existence marks novelty while essence expresses
stability. Yet given the material substratum of sensible creatures,
things can always go wrong, as the focus on individual existents,
rather than essences or kinds, introduces.

That fact represents an initial recognition of the "resistance"
Levenson finds expressed in the pre-existent stuff of the Genesis
story, reminding us how what the creator deems good can fail. Yet
intentional creatures can fail the creator even more directly, by oper-
atively rejecting the relation which links them with existing itself.
We call that failure "malice," and the refusal it embodies "sin."
An intentional rejection becomes the source of malice precisely because
intentional creatures have the role of "vicegerent" of creation, capable
of initiating a return of emanating things to the One from which they
emanate simply by understanding that these things are not free-
standing but, as created, participate in the being of the creator. So to
reject or ignore the very relatedness they are meant to affirm, inviting
them to return to their source, can only distort the very ethos of
created existence. So creation is inevitably bedeviled by failures
endemic to material stuff, or yet more pointedly, by those who turn

aside from the "good" they are able to recognize as their goal. Yet as actively participating in the gift received, it is the very dynamism of existing which allows for failure and even for malice. Rather than eliminating this shadow accompanying creation itself, a robust sense of existing by participation in the creator leaves room for it, even while the shadowy nature resists explanation. Yet while that acknowledgement concedes that the creator is not "all-powerful," an ambiguous talent at best; it hardly implies a "worthy opponent," nor introduces a dualism at the origin of things. At the same time, however, it will recognize that affirming the "goodness" of creation cannot imply transparent luminosity all the way down. Yet that is the argument which Jon Levenson has with his Jewish interlocutor (as well as a plethora of others), an argument which can be accommodated short of outright Manichean or gnostic assertions.

Finally, we find an unexpected crossover in the sixteenth-century Shi'ite philosophical theologian, Mulla Sadra, as he seconds Aquinas's unabashed affirmation of the primacy of *existing* over *essence*, which had certainly been the case with Aristotle, with his Islamic epigone, Avicenna, and with his dedicated commentator, Averroës. To do so, he had to contradict his predecessor and mentor in the Isfahan school, Mir Damad; as well as Suhrawardi, whose philosophical genius fairly initiated *ishrâq* philosophy in Iraq after Averroës. We shall hear more of him in the final chapter on eschatology, for he developed in a lucid manner the intrinsic connection between emanation and the return, a pattern which has been touted as the very structure of Aquinas's *Summa Theologiae*. For now, we need to pursue the different ways in which the unique relation of creatures to the one creator can elicit a founding attitude of trust on the part of intentional creatures.

Notes

1 Portions of this chapter have been adapted from my "Act of Creation and its Theological Consequences," in Thomas Weinandy OFM Cap, Daniel Keating, and John Yocum (eds), *Aquinas on Doctrine* (London: T & T Clarke, 2004), pp. 27–44, with gratitude to the publishers.

2 Robert Sokolowski, *God of Faith and Reason* (Washington, DC: Catholic University of America Press, 1995), pp. 34–36. For a dramatic account of the sinuous journey to Chalcedon, see Thomas Weinandy, *Does God Change?* (Still River, MA: St Bede's, 1985).

3 Sokolowski, *God of Faith and Reason*, p. 37.

4 For an explicitly interfaith appraisal, see David Burrell and Bernard McGinn (eds), *God and Creation* (Notre Dame, IN: University of Notre Dame Press, 1990), with the more recent Castel Gandolpho colloquy: David Burrell, Carlo Cogliati, Janet M. Soskice, and William R. Stoeger (eds), *Creation and the God of Abraham* (Cambridge: Cambridge University Press, 2010).

5 For a narrative sketch of the interaction among key medieval protagonists, see my *Knowing the Unknowable God: Ibn-Sina, Maimonides, Aquinas* (Notre Dame, IN: University of Notre Dame Press, 1986), as well as *Freedom and Creation in Three Traditions* (Notre Dame, IN: University of Notre Dame Press, 1993).

6 Jon Levenson, *Creation and the Persistence of Evil: The Jewish Drama of Divine Omnipotence* (Princeton, NJ: Princeton University Press, 1994).

7 Richard M. Frank, *Creation and the Cosmic System: Al-Ghazâlî and Avicenna* (Heidelberg: Carl Winter, 1992).

8 *Al-Ghazali: The Ninety-Nine Beautiful Names of God* (trans. David Burrell and Nazih Daher; Cambridge: Islamic Texts Society, 1992).

9 *Summa Theologiae* 1.1. Prol.

10 Ian Netton, *Allah Transcendent: Studies in the Structure and Semiotics of Islamic Philosophy, Theology and Cosmology* (London: Routledge, 1989), p. 22. For a critical appreciation of this erudite treatise which calls attention to its pointedness, see Richard Taylor's review in *Middle East Journal* 44 (1990), 521–522.

11 See the reading of Thomas Michel, "God's Covenant with Mankind according to the Qur'an," *Bulletin of the Secretariat for Non-Christians* 52 (1983); reprinted in *Encounter* (Rome) 101 (1983); in *The Catholic Witness* (Ibadan, Nigeria) IV/10 (1983).

12 Levenson, *Creation and the Persistence of Evil*, p. xxv.

13 For a less polemical account which retains the punch of Levenson, see Paul Griffiths, *Intellectual Appetite* (Washington DC: Catholic University of America Press, 2009): "it clearly belongs to the grammar of Christian thought to say that there is almost omnipresent damage, best construed as lack, the absence of particular goods they should have. ..." (p. 90).

2

Relating Divine Freedom with Human Freedom: Diverging and Converging Strategies

Any tradition which accepts the astounding claim that all-that-is emanates freely from one creator cannot but encounter difficulties attempting to articulate that relation in such a way that the One leaves room for the panoply of a diverse created multitude. If it were not for intentional creatures, however, the overwhelming presence of so complex a multitude would relegate this conundrum to the arena of arcane metaphysics: the celebrated "problem of the many and the One." When we consider creatures practicing that freedom which distinguishes them from the rest of creation, however, a free creator can become a daunting presence. We need only recall the way the very notion of a creator who acts freely in originating the universe met resistance from those who found a Plotinian emanation far more intellectually satisfying than the image of a free creator who might well act arbitrarily. So each of these traditions will seek ways to align the creator's exercise of freedom with wisdom rather than with sheer power. The strategies employed will be designed to avoid any semblance of a "zero-sum" game between creator and creatures, since that would presume a creator

Towards a Jewish-Christian-Muslim Theology, First Edition. David B. Burrell.
© 2011 John Wiley & Sons Ltd. Published 2011 by John Wiley & Sons Ltd.

competing for space with creatures, and vice versa. So parsing the way a free creator interacts with the sector of creation comprising intentional creatures becomes the most poignant illustration of the singular "distinction" between creator and creatures.

As we have just seen, this topic will cry out for deft philosophical strategies, lest the very narrative structure of revelation leads us towards a god whose presence can only confront that of human beings, a god poised to compete with free creatures in an utterly unfair contest. So those who unwittingly accept this picture at face value will have to search for ways to remove free creatures from so overwhelming a presence. The name for this tactic in Jewish thought is *tsimtsum*, while the Islamic school called *Mu'tazilite* offered a similar way to exempt, as it were, free agents from the pervasive presence of the creator God. This could not last very long in Islam, however, for it meant withdrawing a large part of the created world from the sovereignty of God. We may easily subvert this potentially idolatrous strategy, however, by exposing the hidden premise: a free action must be utterly free of any antecedents, so mimic creation *ex nihilo*. What results is an autonomy so radical that it inevitably pits creature against creator, but this time by presuming creatures to be on a par with their creator: indeed, creators *ex nihilo*. Yet absent a creator, in a world bereft of purely spiritual beings, like angels, as well, human beings are indeed at the pinnacle, so function effectively like gods. So "moderns" would find this picture attractive, though seldom reflect on its theological import, so it assumes the role of unspoken presumption.[1] So each of these traditions will have to find ways to articulate the elusive relation between creator and creatures so as to avoid competition, as well as delineate an autonomy appropriate to human freedom in a way reflecting their status as creatures.

Mu'tazilite Defense of Human Freedom

Early *Kalam* writers moved quickly to an ontological reading of things, despite the paucity of conceptual tools in their possession.[2]

Reception of the Qur'an had led, understandably enough, to quite disparate views on the relation of human and divine freedom: one which underscored human responsibility for responding to the invitation proffered in the Qur'an; the other which emphasized divine sovereignty.[3] Given the inherently dialectical character of such debates, it is probably unsurprising that a defense of one would utilize the perspectives of the other; those intent on reminding us of the freedom to choose which pervades the Qur'an were dubbed *qadarites* (from the Arabic *qadr* or "power") while those defending divine sovereignty over all of creation were called *jabarites* (from the Arabic *jabr* or "constraint"). Yet a defense of human empowerment to make such momentous decisions about one's destiny took its lead from the dominant picture of divine sovereignty, insisting that a space be cleared within which humans – and *not* God – would be sovereign. Their reasoning in this regard presumed that a free action must effect an absolute beginning, so free human actions were likened to God's activity in creating *ex nihilo*.

Reaction to Mu'tazilites with al-Ghazali's response[4]

It is not hard to see that such a position could not prevail in a tradition which insisted that God is the free creator of all that is. To remove an entire domain from God's creating power – indeed, a domain as extensive as that of free human actions – certainly counters a primary tenet of Islam. So a Mu'tazilite thinker, al-Ash'ari, came to see the light, and played a major role in developing an alternative position which proposed to preserve both human responsibility and divine sovereignty. Yet he too was constrained by the paradigm of full-fledged free action as amounting to creation *ex nihilo*, so offered an intermediate status for human actions according to which human beings *perform* the actions which God *creates*; we play, in other words, scripted parts.[5] Al-Ghazali subscribed to the view originally proposed by al-Ash'ari, which had become the accepted position in Islam, although (as we shall see) he could not permit himself to restrict *acting* to *creating*. Nonetheless, creating remained for him as well the prime analogate for the term "act," susceptible as it is of diverse uses, so he can insist that the key to a proper stance in Islamic philosophical theology lies in affirming that "there is no agent but God most high."[6]

Developing this key statement in relation to human agents, Ghazali will align himself with al-Ash'ari in principle, yet refuse to rest with resolutions which seem mostly verbal, or with a merely "ontological" account of human action. His way of illustrating *tawhid*, the central faith conviction of Islam, as "there is no agent but God most high" involves (1) reminding us that "agent" is a multivalent term, and (2) probing the convoluted path of *willing* in humans. With regard to our use of "agent" he remarks:

> If human beings are agents, how is it that God most high is an agent? Or if God most high is an agent, how is a human being an agent? There is no way of understanding "acting" as between these two agents. In response, I would say: indeed, there can be no understanding when there is but one meaning for "agent". But if it had two meanings, then the term comprehended could be attributed to each of them without contradiction, as when it is said that the emir killed someone, and also said that the executioner killed him; in one sense, the emir is the killer and in another sense, the executioner. Similarly, a human being is an agent in one sense, and God – great and glorious – is an agent in another. The sense in which God most high is agent is that He is the originator,[7] the one who brings about existence [*al-mukhtari' al-mawjud*], while the sense in which a human being is an agent is that he is the locus [*mahal*] in which power is created after will has been created after knowledge has been created, so that power depends on will, and movement is linked to power, as a conditioned to its condition.[8] But depending on the power of God is the dependence of effect on cause, of the originated on the origina-tor. So everything which depends on a power in such a way as it is the locus of the power is called "agent" in a manner which expresses that fact of its dependence, much as the executioner can be called "killer" and the emir a killer, since the killing depends on the power of both of them, yet in different respects. In that way both of them are called "killer", and similarly, the things ordained [*maqrûrât*] depend on two powers. (p. 40)

Ghazali's constructive view of the hidden pathways of human motivation involves an extended parable in which the pilgrim is taken
on a journey through the "worlds" which are invisible from the
sensible world yet which regulate its activity:

> This servant, the pilgrim, returned and apologized for his questions
> and his censures, saying to the right hand, the pen, understanding,
> will, power, and the rest: "Accept my apologies, for I am a stranger
> only recently arrived in this land, and anyone who comes here is
> perplexed. I was resisting only because of my limitations and my
> ignorance. Now it is only right for me to apologize to you as it has
> been unveiled to me that the One who alone [possesses] the earthly
> world, the intelligible world, majesty and power, is the One, the
> Dominator.[9] And all of you are in His service, under His domination
> and His power, continually in His grasp – He is the First and the Last,
> the Manifest and the Hidden" (Q 57:3)".[10] If anyone repeats that in
> the visible world people will consider it far-fetched and say to him:
> "How can something be first and last, for these two attributes are
> opposed to one another? For what is first is not last, and what is
> manifest is not hidden". To which he will respond: He is first with
> respect to existing things, for they all emanate from Him one after
> another in an ordered fashion; and He is last with respect to initiating
> undertakings, for they will only continue to progress from one stage
> to another in such as way as to arrive at their goal in His presence.
> So He is the last point on [their] journey, which makes Him the last
> in the visible world and the first in existence. Correlatively, He is
> hidden from those taken up with the visible world, seeking to per-
> ceive Him with their five senses, yet manifest to those who seek Him
> by the light which kindles in their hearts, by an inner vision which
> offers a hidden opening to the intelligible world. This is what faith
> in divine unity consists in for those actively journeying on the path
> of such faith; that is, those to whom it has been unveiled that there
> is but one agent. (pp. 28–29)

Ghazali then offers a description of the interrelation of willing and
discerning which elicits the objection:

> Now you may say: this is sheer constraint [*jabr*] and constraint is in
> direct opposition to freedom of choice [*ikhtiyâr*]. And you do not deny

freedom of choice, so how can those who are constrained also freely choose? To which I would respond: if the covering were unveiled, you would recognize that there is constraint in the course of freedom of choice, in such a way that it is itself constrained to choose. But how can you comprehend this when you do not understand freedom of choice? So let us explain freedom of choice in the language of the theologians, but in a concise manner so as neither to intrude nor inconvenience, since the aim of this book is only the understanding of religious practice. I can say that the language of action is applied to human beings in three ways. Hence it is said: a man writes with fingers, breathes with lungs and his neck cleaves water when his body comes in to relation with it, in such a way that cleaving the water is attributed to him, as is breathing and writing. Yet these three are one in the essential reality of necessity and constraint, although they differ in ways other than that, which I shall clarify for you from three vantage points.

We call his cleaving water, insofar as it happens to him, in this respect a natural action; while we call his breathing a voluntary action [*irâdîan*], and his writing a freely chosen action [*ikhtiyârîan*]. Constraint is evident in natural action insofar as something happens to the surface of the water so that it overflows into the air, inevitably cleaving the air, so that the cleaving necessarily happens after the overflowing. It is similar with breathing, for the movement of the throat is related to wanting to breathe as the cleaving of the water is related to the weight of the body; since where there is weight there is cleaving in the wake of it, so where there is no willing there is no breathing. In a similar way, if one aims a pin at a person's eye, he will close his eyelids of necessity, and were he to want to hold them open he could not, even though this necessary shutting of the eyelids is an intentional action. Moreover, if the point of a pin were presented to one's perception, this necessary wanting to close [one's eyelids] would occur along with the movement; and were one to want to resist that, he would not be able to, even though it is an action of the power and the will. For the fact that this action is connected with natural action makes it necessary.

So for the third form of action, that of free choice, it is an ambiguous notion like writing and speaking. For of free choice it is said that one wills to do it or one wills not to do it, or sometimes, that one does not will at all; thereby imagining that one knows how matters lie, but in fact only manifesting one's ignorance of the meaning of freedom of choice. So let us remove the veil from it to explain it. Freedom of choice follows upon the understanding that judges whether a thing is appropriate for you, for things are divided into what your outer or inner perception judges, without confusion or uncertainty, to be right for you, notably regarding those things about which reason has hitherto been indecisive. For you determine without hesitation [what to do] when someone, for example, aims a pin at your eye or a sword at your body, nor have you any uncertainty realizing that you should repel them for your own good and benefit. And it is hardly wrong for the will to be aroused by reason or the power by the will, or for the eyelids to be put into motion by a thrust, or the hand moved by a sword thrust – yet without any deliberation or reflection. So it is with the will.

There are things, however, about which discrimination and reason remain undecided, without being able to discern whether they are appropriate or not, so that one needs to deliberate and reflect whether it is better to do them or to let them pass. When after reflection and deliberation reason decides upon one of these courses of action, it prefers connecting that with what it determined without reflection or deliberation. At this point the will is aroused just as it is aroused by the thrust of a sword or the tip of a spear. So we call this will [*irâda*] which is aroused to action by what appears good to reason, "freedom of choice" [*ikhtiyâr*], as it craves the good [*al-khaîr*]. By that I mean that it is aroused by what appears to reason to be good for it, which is the source of this will. Nor does this will need to wait to be aroused by what it is expecting, for it is an evident good with respect to action, differing from the evident good in [resisting] the thrust of the sword only in that this took place spontaneously without any reflection while the other required reflection (pp. 32–34).

After these extensive preliminaries, we are led to a constructive account of human freedom:

So freedom of choice consists in a specific willing which is aroused by a counsel of reason which also, once perceived, brings it to its term. It is said about this [process] that reason is required for it to distinguish which is the better of two goods or the lesser of two evils. We cannot conceive the will being aroused except by movement of the senses or the imagination, or by a decisive movement on the part of reason. As a result, if someone wanted, for example, to slit his own throat, he would not be able to do so – not for want of power in his hand nor for lack of a knife, but because the personal will to motivate the power is not present.[11] And the will is not present because it is not aroused by the movement of reason or the evident advantage of doing the appropriate action. Indeed, since killing himself is not an action appropriate for him, he remains unable to do it, despite the strength in his arms to kill himself – without bringing on a reaction so distressing that he could not bear it. In this case, reason withholds judgment and hesitates, because it is in doubt regarding which of the two evils is worse, yet if after reflection it thinks it better to refrain from killing, as the lesser evil, then it is not possible for him to kill himself. Yet if he should judge that killing is the lesser evil, and if his judgment is decisive – no longer simply inclining towards it nor turning away from it – then the will and the power will be aroused and he will destroy himself.

Such a person would then be like someone whom one was pursuing with a sword to kill him. Supposing that he threw himself from a roof and so met his end, [that action itself] would not have occurred to him nor would he have been able not to throw himself down. [On the other hand], if someone pursued him with light blows and he were to arrive at the edge of the roof, reason would judge that the blows were of less significance than the prospect of jumping off, so his limbs would bring him to a stop and he would not be able to throw himself down. For no motivation to do so would be aroused, since the motivation of the will is subservient to the judgment of reason and the senses, while the power is subservient to the motivation, and movement to the power, and all of it is decreed necessarily to an extent to which one is quite unaware. A human being is but the locus and channel for these things, so it could not be the case that they would be from him.[12] So the meaning of his being constrained results from the fact that all of this is produced in him from outside him and not from himself, and the meaning of his being free to choose consists in his being the place in which the will originates in him what is constrained by the judgment of reason: that an action be unqualifiedly good and fitting; so the judgment which emerges is also constrained. As a result he is indeed constrained with regard to freedom of choice. Yet the action of fire in burning, for example, is unqualifiedly one of constraint, while the action of God the most high represents unqualified freedom of choice. So the action of a human being, while it may be constrained in freedom of choice, is on a level between these two (pp. 35–36).

But how can we find a place between natural activity and divine action, between unqualified constraint and unqualified freedom of choice, and how ought we describe it if we can? Yet in fact, locating such a place will be consequent upon finding an appropriate description for it. Ghazali's response is to clarify the grammar of the matter, and then direct us to practice, as the title of this book from his magnum opus, the *Ihyâ 'Ulum ad-Din*, displays its two connected parts: "The Book of Faith in Divine Unity [*Tawhîd*] and Trust in Divine Providence [*Tawakkul*]."

Yet in the measure that the truth is revealed to those inquiring, they will know that things are quite the opposite, and they will say: O linguist, you have posited the term "agent" to signify the one who originates, but [in that sense] there is no agent but God, so the term belongs properly to Him and metaphorically to whatever is other than Him. That is, you must bear with the way in which linguists have determined it. When the authentic meaning happened to roll off the tongue of a certain Arab [Bedouin], whether intentionally or by chance, the messenger of God gave him his due, saying: "The most apt verse ever spoken by a poet is the saying of Labid: 'But for everything, what is without God is nothing''. That is, everything which does not subsist in itself, but has its subsistence from another, from the point of view of itself, is nothing. For its truth and its reality comes from another and not from itself, so it is not true essentially [*lâ haqq bihaqîqa*] outside "the living and the subsisting [One]" (Q 2:255, 3:2), to Whom "there is no likeness" (Q 42:11), for He subsists essentially [*bidhâtihi*] while everything that is other than Him subsists by His power. So He is the truly real One [*al-Haqq*] and all that is other than Him is nothing.[13] As Sahl [al-Tustarî] said: "O poor man! He was and you were not, and He will be and you will not be. While you are today, you say: 'I'; be now as though you had not been, for He is today as He was".

You may still object: it is now clear that all is coerced [*jabr*]. But if so, what can these mean: reward or punishment, anger or complete approval [*ridâ'*]?[14] How can He be angry at His own deed? You should know that we have already indicated the meaning of that in the Book of Thanksgiving [Book 32 of the *Ihyâ'*], so we will not proceed to a long repetition here. For this has to do with the divine decree [*qadar*], intimations of which we saw with respect to the faith in divine unity which brings about the state of trust in divine providence, and is only perfected by faith in the benevolence and wisdom [of God]. And if faith in divine unity brings about insight into the effects of causes, abundant faith in benevolence is what brings about confidence in the effects of the causes, and the state of trust in divine providence will only be perfected, as I shall relate, by confidence in the guarantor [*wakîl*] and tranquillity of heart towards the benevolent oversight of the [divine] sponsor. For this faith is indeed an exalted chapter in the chapters of faith, and the stories about it from the path of those experiencing the unveiling go on at length. So let us simply mention it briefly: to wit, the conviction of the seeker in the station of faith in divine unity, a conviction held firmly and without any doubt. This is a faith deemed to be trustworthy and certain, with no weakness or doubt accompanying it, that when God – great and glorious – created all human beings according to a reason greater than reason and an understanding greater than their understanding, that He also created for them an understanding that would sustain each one of them, and bestowed on them a wisdom that they would never cease describing. (pp. 43–45)

That wisdom is not available to those who merely speculate; it is reserved for the pilgrims who undertake the journey of trusting in divine providence. What sort of a practice is *tawakkul*: trust in divine providence? It entails accepting whatever happens as part of the inscrutable decree of a just and merciful God. Yet such an action cannot be reduced to mere *resignation*, and so caricatured as "Islamic fatalism." It rather entails aligning oneself with things as they really are: in Ghazali's terms, with the truth that there is no agent but God most high. This requires effort since we cannot formulate the relationship between this single divine agent and the other agents which we know, and also because things as we understand them to be are not *true*: human society lives under the sign of *jâhiliyya* or pervasive ignorance. Yet the effort cannot be solely an intellectual one; that is, I cannot learn "the truth" in such a way as to align myself with it, in the time-honored fashion in which speculative reason is supposed to illuminate practical judgment – for the all-important relationship between these disparate agents resists our formulation. Nevertheless, by trying our best to act according to the conviction that the divine decree expresses the truth in events as they unfold, we are *shown* how things truly lie. So faith [*tawhid*] and practice [*tawakkul*] are reciprocal; neither is foundational. The understanding we can have is that of one journeying in faith, a *salîk*, which is the name which Sufis characteristically appropriated for themselves.

So there is a school of learning how to respond to what happens in such a way that we are shown how things are truly ordered. This school will involve learning from others more practiced in responding rightly, so Ghazali's judicious use of stories is intended to intimate the Sufi practice of master/disciple wherein the novice is helped to discern how to act. There is no higher wisdom – called "philosophy"; speculative reason is wholly subject to practical reason, but that is the inevitable implication of replacing the emanation scheme with an intentional creator![15] So the challenge of understanding the relation of the free creator to the universe becomes the task of rightly responding to events as they happen, in such a way that the true ordering of things – the divine decree – can be made manifest in one's actions-as-responses. Ghazali expresses this relationship between speculative and practical reason by noting that we need to call upon both *knowledge* and *state* in guiding our actions according to a wholehearted trust in God. What he wishes to convey by those terms in tandem is an awareness of the very structure of the book itself: the *knowledge* which faith in divine unity brings can, by dint of sustained practice, lead one to a habitual capacity to align one's otherwise errant responses to situation after situation according to that faith. In short, what Ghazali terms a *state*, relying here on a Sufi anthropology, would be more familiar to Western readers as Aristotle's stable "second nature" of virtue. It is not, to be sure, tied to the Hellenic paradigm of "the magnanimous man," but to a Qur'anic faith. This is even more evident in his treatise on the names of God, for it is the 99 names culled from the Qur'an, names by which God reveals the many "faces" of the divine, which offer a composite picture for human perfection. That book can be read, then, not only as a condensed summary of Islamic theology but also as an Islamic counterpart to Aristotle's *Ethics*. But enough said about Ghazali as an Islamic philosophical theologian. If he tends to resolve to mystical insight in places where philosophers would prefer conceptual schemes, we should recognize that he is gesturing thereby that certain domains quite outstrip human conceptualizing, so that what appears to be a weakness may indeed be the fruit of astute judgment. Even more significant, however, is that everything he says about practice can be carried out quite independently of such "mystical insight," as indeed it must be for the vast majority of faithful.

From Islamic Discussion to Christian Debates contrasting Aquinas with Scotus

What can we gain from this debate and from Ghazali's manner of resolving it? We could begin to ask ourselves whether *choosing* deserves to be taken as the paradigm for free human actions. Or is there a more fundamental level of accepting or rejecting what one deems to be the case with oneself and with the world of which one is a part? On this model, such counsel or discernment would better explicate the freedom which we have, rather than invoking some autonomous agency within us unbeholden to history, embodiment, attractions or compulsions. Indeed these factors seem to represent the stuff of whatever capacity we do have to direct our own lives and be responsible for our actions.[16] Historical, in that freedom is not a mere on/off affair, but that we can be more or less free in the way we negotiate our lives; we can grow in freedom. Embodied, in that factors like gender and class contribute to our being more or less responsible in what we do. Compulsions and attractions, as we shall see, form the warp and woof of an account of progressive freedom, where awareness of the compulsions driving us allows us to negotiate them more or less adequately, while we are called to discriminate among the attractions so as to order them fruitfully. Such a picture of freedom could be described as negotiating between constraint and sheer origination, between determinism, if you will, and utter autonomy; yet allowing us to take responsibility for our actions without thereby insisting that I am my own creation.

Moreover, such a picture of "situated freedom" would allow us to be grateful for all the help we receive, even from our creator! Note also that the creator's assistance will not be constraining, because the agencies involved are not competitive. Here Aquinas's serene remarks that God alone can move the will without constraining it (*Summa Theologiae* (ST) 1.111.2) reinforce Ghazali from a more articulate perspective: "to be moved voluntarily is to be moved of one's own accord, i.e., from a resource within. That inner resource, however, may derive from some other, outward source. In this sense there is no contradiction between being moved of one's own accord and being moved by another" – so long as that "other" be the creator of all things (ST 1.105.4.2). For the creator of all, on Aquinas's metaphysical account, bestows the "act of being" (*esse*) which is "more intimately and profoundly interior to things than anything else" (ST 1.8.1), so such a One can only be called "external" to the creature in a unique sense determined by the original "distinction" of creature from the creator.[17] This observation parallels Ghazali's coupling his insistence that "there is no agent but God most high" with the reminder that we cannot hope to know – in the sense of being able speculatively to articulate – the relation between that originating and sustaining agency and our derived agency. Moreover, it is the counsel of both these thinkers that the only understanding available to us will be that acquired by the pilgrim: theory gives way to practice – a practice which can give each person intent upon the way a privileged access, but *not* of a Cartesian sort, and communicable to others only though their way of living.

Beyond these positioning remarks, what can we learn by considering Ghazali's efforts to articulate human freedom as they reflect a tradition which takes as its initial premise the free creation of the universe by one God? First, that the impulse to secure human freedom by removing it from divine sovereignty is a nonstarter if we are to be faithful to the grounding insight of such traditions. Next, that we can avoid many a false conundrum by distinguishing among diverse senses of "agent," which should then allow us to become aware of any tendency to assimilate free and responsible agents to the creator by demanding that they be utterly "unmoved movers." Finally, that a positive articulation of human freedom in such a context will prove at once difficult and illuminating. Difficult, in that it seems to ask us to conceptualize the relation of the One creator to us creatures; illuminating, in that it opens us to an understanding of the trajectories of human freedom which gives full recognition to the realities of human action as we engage in it. If we think of those realities in the way just mentioned, as "pushes" or "pulls," we shall see that a full contextualization of created agents in relation to their creator will offer us ways of neutralizing the *pushes* and of ordering the *pulls* along a path which promises yet greater freedom.

For in an account which locates the origins of human freedom in humankind's free creation in the "image and likeness" of its creator, freedom (like existing) will not be a simple "on/off" property, but will rather demand to be treated as a capacity which we are called to exercise Yet it will remain as much aspiration as achievement in us, given the obstacles – the "pushes" as well as our inveterate tendency to self-deception – which bedevil it in practice.[18] The fresh perspective such traditions offer can also help us to see how purely "metaphysical" accounts, like that of early *Kalam* or contemporary "could do otherwise" paradigms, show themselves to be too remote from the contextual realities to prove very illuminating. We need "thicker descriptions" of human action, as critics of "alternative possibility" accounts of human freedom have reminded us.[19] Reflection on literary sources, to take a salient example, can sensitize us to the more and less of human freedom; ideally, to the progressive realization of freedom through a person's life-journey, as exquisitely displayed in Dante's pilgrim. And these rich perspectives can remind us that a simple binary opposition of freedom/determinism will inevitably fail to capture the realities involved.

The perspective of created freedom – that is, free creatures freely created – can also alert us to infelicities in standard "libertarian" accounts, the nub of which can be found in the opening lines of Roderick Chisholm's Lindley lecture (1964), where the key issue of personal responsibility is parsed as demanding that "what was to happen at the time of the [action] was something that was entirely up to the man himself."[20] Responsibility – "the buck stops here" – is certainly the key, yet everything turns on what we deem that to require. If it entails being "prime movers unmoved," then Chisholm effectively assumes a Mu'tazilite position: "if we are responsible ... then we have a prerogative which some would attribute only to God: each of us, when we act, is a prime mover unmoved" (p. 32). Yet such an assertion ought to be off-putting to believer and unbeliever alike, albeit for opposite reasons: believers, for removing a considerable domain of creation from the sovereignty of its creator; and unbelievers, for postulating that utterly autonomous agents had managed to emerge from the natural landscape. Again, a glance at the efforts of those who have preceded us, and the dialectic among opposing positions on this elusive issue, may illuminate us. Chisholm's allusion to an *actus elicitus* of the will (p. 32) is a legacy from John Duns Scotus's attempt to establish *will* as an agent in its own right, independent of the intellect whose counsel it needs.[21] Motivated, it seems, by the condemnations of 1277, and perhaps stimulated by rivalries between Dominicans and Franciscan, Scotus sought to enshrine human freedom in a self-moving faculty – the will – which could itself "elicit" acts. Effectively separated from "outside" influences like discernment, human responsibility was secured by making the will a first mover. This perspective received new life in a fresh polemical context from Kant: virtue, if it really be virtue, must reside in the will alone; only wills can be good. It is this stream which has fostered "libertarian" accounts of human freedom.

It may focus our alternative by contrasting Scotus's account with that of Thomas Aquinas, whom he often criticized. Where Aquinas considers *will* in the line of nature, Scotus opposes the freedom of will to the necessity of nature; where Aquinas expounds willing by analogy with reasoning and relies on the complementarity of these parallel intellectual faculties to construct the dynamics of willing as a moved movement, Scotus gives manifest priority to will as an unmoved (or "autonomous") mover. (This summary statement would be contested immediately by Scotus scholars, and I have tried to take their objections and nuances into consideration in what follows, as a way of signaling my gratitude for their helping us trace the subtleties of the "subtle doctor."[22]) Indeed, one need not construe these considerable differences as polarizing these two thinkers on the subject of human freedom, for they do "agree on the fundamental tenet that, ultimately, in a free choice it is an act of will that settles which alternative will be pursued," yet that characterization is so general that it can be misleading.[23] What separates them, it seems, is a diverse set of preoccupations, proximate among which must be counted the condemnations of 1277, which arose in part because some were not as careful as Aquinas in explicating the intellect's relation to willing.[24] Yet they divide even more saliently in their respective ways of conceiving the relation of creature to its creator.

With regard to our relation to God as our creator, Aquinas had found Aristotle's conception of natures with inbuilt aims to be a useful conceptual tool for elaborating the activity of intentional beings Once seen to be created in the image of their maker, their natures would be oriented to that same One as their goal, yet that goal would only be realized through their free activity. (This activity will in turn become a *response* in the light of divine grace.) Moreover, the Aristotelian principle, "whatever is in motion is moved by another," offered Aquinas a way of showing how the dependence of such beings on the One originating them could be incorporated into that very activity: the inbuilt orientation together with the initial "specification" of the will by that One to "the good" accounts for the will's ability to originate activity, without however determining the outcome of any choice. For the "comprehensive good" is not itself something chosen; yet whatever is chosen will be a means to this or lesser ends subordinate to it. And even in these choices, while the will may be specified (or "informed") by what one perceives to be best for one, the action itself flows from the action of the will; so "for Aquinas as well as for Scotus, there are no *sufficient* conditions of the choice antecedent to the choice itself."[25]

Yet that activity will always be conceived, for Aquinas, as the activity of a creature in the manner we have sketched; whereas for Scotus, it will be affirmed to be such, but conceived as the activity of a creature endowed with a capacity to originate activity, which enables it to "cooperate" with the divine will in a fully free act, which would direct it to its true end.[26] Indeed, the notion of cooperation (or "concurrence") represents Scotus's mature position on the relation of intellect and will in producing a free act, with the intellect (as a "natural agent") subordinated to the inherently free activity of the will "to elicit an act."[27] Yet once the created agent is deemed to be autonomous, precisely to guarantee its capacity of initiation, then creature and creator will be conceived in parallel, the divine activity will be termed "concursus," and the stage is set for a zero-sum game in which one protagonist's gain is the other's loss. Theologically, the polarities observed in Islamic *kalam* cannot help but emerge: either creatures freely initiate their actions absent divine influence or they "acquire" (or "perform") actions created by God. Metaphysically, one will find oneself drawn to a "possibilism" in which such "agents" will be conceivable "before" they are created, so that the creator can envisage which "ones" it is fitting to cooperate with. The affinity with such a metaphysical position stems from the initial propensity to conceive creator and creatures in parallel or by way of simple contrast – which turn out to be the same thing.[28] Such a perspective effectively elides the unique founding relation, creation, best elucidated by a metaphysics which can understand *act* analogously, and so indicate how the originating activity of the creator continues to make the creature to be an agent in its own right. Aquinas puts this elegantly when he transforms the emanation scheme to schematize the providential care of a free creator: "divine providence works through intermediaries ... not through any impotence on [God's] part, but from the abundance of [divine] goodness imparting to creatures also the dignity of causing" (ST 1.22.3).

From Philosophical to Literary Witnesses

This austere image of freedom quite separated from wider reaches of human motivation, initiated by Scotus and elaborated by Kant, also inspired Milton's image of the center of hell as a raging fire: passion overwhelming duty, the mainspring of Puritan morality. The completely opposite image at the center of Dante's *Inferno* offers a dramatic alternative: a lake of ice cutting off all possibility of responding to any solicitation at all. The literary structure of pilgrimage allows these images to be just that for us: images, warnings and contrastive illuminations of the authentic path. For the reaches of human freedom are displayed in sinners as well as in saints: abusing it can lead to its irrevocable loss, while exercising it can enhance our personal possession of it. Putting things this way, however, reminds us how this alternative to Scotus represents a normative conception of freedom. For if freedom is located simply in choosing, if our glory as free creatures consists in being total self-starters, then discussions of it will focus on that fact alone. Whether the resulting actions lead to our demise or our flourishing will be a separate matter. But if we find so unrelenting a focus on choice distorts the intimate relation between human freedom and ethics, then understanding our actions will necessarily involve their trajectory as well. That, I take it, is what people tend to mean by "a normative view of freedom." Nietzsche and Jean-Paul Sartre have helped us to clarify the polarities here: are we setting out to make ourselves or are we responding to a call?

Put this way, the position and role of a free creator enters as energizing our freedom rather than presenting itself as a dominating threat to it (even though it seems that Sartre could never rid himself of the latter image). For the action of such a creator terminates in natures whose inbuilt *telos* will be to return to their origin, while leaving open yet another level of interaction which can invite individuals so natured to respond to this call in such a way that these same human capacities are wondrously enhanced – the traditional distinction in Christian theology of *natural* from *supernatural*. While it was Aquinas, as we have seen, who fleshed out this picture of freedom, capitalizing on Aristotle's mean/ends analysis, and clarifying Augustine's understanding of *will* as a "moved mover," Dante's poetic assimilation of this detailed analysis offers our most humane access to it. In a similar way, Gandhi's insistence that means must be related internally to the ends they serve can help forestall many misunderstandings which the Aristotelian analysis may provoke.[29] We may now be in a position to see how elevating *choice* to the paradigm of freedom actually succeeds in distorting it. On an Aristotelian account, rooted in his conviction of the inherent *telos* of natures, an orientation Aquinas will ground in those natures emanating from the activity of a free creator, choosing concerns means whereas ends are either consented to or refused, connected as they are with our very nature. Furthermore, means and ends are related Chinese-box style, so that most ends also become means in relation to further goals, with the result that there is a great deal of choosing to be done.

Yet that orienting activity which discerns proper ends and consents to them is not accurately called a "choice." Indeed, Jean-Paul Sartre's insistence that it must be a choice displays that fact, for he explicitly positions himself in opposition to this entire scheme of "natures." Yet while that activity is not fruitfully described as a "choice," the alternative of failing to consent to the recognized *telos* of one's nature, articulated in revelation perspectives as the creator's call, remains always present for human beings. To this extent, Thomas Aquinas could be called a "libertarian": human beings can be utterly autonomous and the human will can be an unmoved mover, but only in *rejecting* one's destiny. Yet human creatures can only accomplish that in an indirect fashion, by allowing ourselves to be distracted from our proper end by various forms of self-deception.[30] So Aquinas could hardly make that self-destructive "activity" paradigmatic for human freedom. Choosing cannot be paradigmatic for human freedom since choice, properly speaking, regards means and not ends. And we either consent to or refuse ends – when they are discerned as ends. This insight, which flows logically from an Aristotelian means/ends analysis, invites us to ponder whether the most significant decisions in our life are best described as "choices." Do people *choose* their spouses, perhaps out of a field of contenders? Or even if one might be tempted to see one's action this way, especially in societies which have been described as "tyrannized by choice," is the decisive move completely "up to me?" Is it not rather that our significant life-decisions call for more discernment than choice, asking that we accept or reject what we have come to recognize about ourselves and about the situation in which we find ourselves?[31]

There are alternatives, certainly, but not *choices*; or perhaps better, choosing at such a point would be irrational. We tend rather to say: "I have no choice in it." Similar things could be said about "choosing" our path in life. In fact, we are imbedded in fields of force, some of which push and others of which pull us. We are, it seems, even phenomenologically, at best "moved movers," and we function at our best as we identify and compensate for the "pushes" or compulsions, and learn to respond – in an ordered fashion – to the "pulls" or goals. The ordering involves ranking these attractions as priorities, in such a way that the larger and more momentous ones encompass the lesser, in Chinese-box fashion, so that any deviation from such an ordering can fairly be defined as a seduction. On this account, an authentic human path becomes one which aligns itself with the relative worth of the goals it pursues, internalizing them as motivators by trial and error. In the presence of a free creator, our activity then aims to return all that we have received to the One from whom we have received it all – the operative sense of the term "islam" in Muslim life and teaching. Aquinas's understanding of our very existence as a free gift from God as well as the source of all that I might do, for action follows upon being, delineates how the activity of sorting our goals and pursuing them roots human freedom more in discernment than choice, more in contemplation or vision than in "deciding."[32]

On such an account, while we humans may be a privileged part of the universe in being able to recognize, discriminate among, and order the goals presented to us as attractions, we nonetheless remain, in our natures, as goal-oriented as the rest of nature. This reality about us is most clearly demonstrated, tragically enough, in its absence: in depression, where one can feel little or no motivation to do anything. Or by its perversion, sin, where our endemic capacity for self-deception keeps us from calling things by their proper names and so inhibits our ordering prospective actions in a scheme which bears any relation to how things really are. At root, then, this scheme shared by Christian and Muslim traditions finds freedom exercised paradigmatically in accepting our God-given natures as part of the cosmos, rather than in choosing to stand out as an autonomous actor whose primary goal must lie in being one's own creator.

Summary Remarks

Perhaps the earlier controversy within *kalam* will have helped us to grasp differences cognate with those in Christian medieval discussion regarding created human freedom. I have tried to indicate ways in which both discussions turn on the conception one has of God as creator and the way in which one then goes on to delineate our status as creatures. If initiating activity in such a way as to claim responsibility for that action must be identified with utter origination, then there would seem to be no place for a properly subordinate agent. Yet the doctrine of creation, as understood by Jews, Christians, and Muslims alike, clearly entails that creatures are subordinate to the creator in all that they are and do. So we need to discover the philosophical tools to craft such an agent. This is precisely what Aquinas's transformation of Aristotle's elucidation of human agency has done. If the means/ends analysis appears at first glance to be too complex, it must be compared to other analyses or mere assertions about human freedom, like "the capacity to do otherwise." Indeed, what commends Aquinas's account is the way we can employ it to help us understand the dynamics of our own action. In that sense, it can best be dubbed a "constructive analysis." Similarly, to be free and to exercise our inherent freedom does not require that we be autonomous, total initiators of our own actions, but rather that we respond discerningly to the attractions which beset us: responding at best to those which lead us expansively to that one good to which we cannot help but be attracted. A final word: if the foregoing arguments strike one as more rhetorical than probative, that is what they are meant to be. I have been persuaded by John Milbank, in his *Theology and Social Theory*, that arguments in favor of one telling perspective over another cannot in principle be probative, but must perforce be rhetorical in character.[33] Yet what such arguments can accomplish is to remind us of the *point* of our philosophical inquiries, and that may prove to have a usefulness well beyond argument.

Notes

1 See Alvin Plantinga's "free will defense" in *Nature of Necessity* (Oxford: Clarendon Press, 1974); Jonathan Kvanvig puts it succinctly: "no action is free unless brought about *only* by the agent himself" (*The Possibility of an All-Knowing God* (New York: St Martin's Press, 1986), p. 119, emphasis added), cited in Gerard F. O'Hanlon, SJ, *The Immutablity of God in the Theology of Hans Urs von Balthasar* (Cambridge: Cambridge University Press, 1990), pp. 158, 160.

2 Richard Frank is an astute and reliable guide to these matters; see his "Moral Obligation in Classical Muslim Theology," *Journal of Religious Ethics* 11 (1983), 204–223.

3 William Montgomery Watt has canvassed this debate in *Free Will and Predestination in Early Islam* (London: Luzac, 1948).

4 This section has been adapted from my *Faith and Freedom* (Oxford: Blackwell, 2004), Ch. 11, pp. 158–166.

5 See my development of *kasb* in *Freedom and Creation in Three Traditions* (Notre Dame, IN: University of Notre Dame Press, 1993), pp. 79–83; for a comprehensive view see Daniel Gimaret, *La Doctrine d'al-Ash'ari* (Paris: Cerf, 1990).

6 Citations from al-Ghazali are taken from my translation: *Book of Faith in Divine Unity and Trust in Divine Providence (Kitâb at-Tawhîd wa Tawakkul)* from the *Ihya' 'Ulum ad-Dîn* (Louisville, KY: Fons Vitae, 2001). Citation at p. 15, following page numbers in text.

7 This term is not Qur'anic nor is it a name of God; cf. L.P. Fitzgerald, *Creation in al-Tafsîr al-Kabîr of Fakhr ad-Din al-Razi* (PhD dissertation, Australian National University, 1992), p. 34.

8 Cf. Richard Frank, *Creation and the Cosmic System: al-Ghazâlî and Avicenna* (Heidelberg: Carl Winter, 1992), p. 25.

9 Divine names; cf. *Al-Ghazali: The Ninety-Nine Beautiful Names of God* (trans. David Burrell and Nazih Daher; Cambridge: Islamic Texts Society, 1992), p. 74.

10 Divine names; cf. *Al-Ghazali: The Ninety-Nine Beautiful Names*, pp. 133–137, which the following closely parallels.

11 The expression here translated as "motivate" (*dâ'iah*) is treated extensively in Daniel Gimaret, *Théories de l'acte humain en théologie musulmane* (Paris: Vrin, 1980), *passim*, see Index des Termes Techniques 407.

12 Again, for an account of this "theory of action" involving such "motivations [dâ'iah]" see Gimaret, *Théories de l'acte humain*, esp. pp. 143–148, and also Richard M. Frank, "The Autonomy of the Human Agent in the Teaching of 'Abd al-Jabbar," *Le Muséon* 95 (1982), 323–355, as well as his review of Gimaret in *Biblioteche Orientalis* 39 (1982), 705–715.

13 Divine name; cf. *Al-Ghazali: The Ninety-Nine Beautiful Names*, pp. 124–126.

14 For the sense of *rîdâ'*, see Marie-Louise Siauve's translation of *Kitâb al-hubb* of the *Ihây': Livre de l'amour* (Paris: Vrin, 1986), pp. 247–268.

15 Cf. my "Why Not Pursue the Metaphor of Artisan and View God's Knowledge as Practical?" in Lenn E. Goodman (ed.), *Neoplatonism and Jewish Thought* (Albany, NY: State University of New York Press, 1992), pp. 207–216.

16 I am indebted here to Joseph Incandela's doctoral dissertation: "Aquinas' Lost Legacy: God's Practical Knowledge and Situated Human Freedom" (Princeton University, 1986).

17 For this sense of "the distinction" see Robert Sokolowski, *The God of Faith and Reason* (Notre Dame, IN: University of Notre Dame Press, 1982; Washington, DC: Catholic University of America Press, 1995), *passim*; Aquinas's treatment of these two freedoms is analyzed more closely in my *Freedom and Creation*, pp. 86–94, where I am expressly

beholden to the now classic account of Bernard Lonergan, *Grace and Freedom* (London: Darton, Longman and Todd, 1971).

18 Christopher Hughes, *On a Complex Theory of a Simple God* (Ithaca, NY: Cornell University Press, 1989), offers an illustration of how attempts to assimilate Aquinas's understanding of *existing* to a contemporary "on/off" notion lead one to miss his central point, see pp. 27–28, 83.

19 See, among others, Eleonore Stump, "Intellect, Will, and the Principle of Alternate Possibilities," in John Martin Fischer (ed.), *Perspectives on Moral Responsibility* (Ithaca, NY: Cornell University Press, 1993), amplified in her recent *Aquinas* (New York: Routledge, 2002), Ch. 9 "Freedom: Action, Intellect and Will."

20 Roderick Chisholm, "*Human Freedom and the Self,*" in Gary Watson (ed.), *Free Will* (New York: Oxford University Press, 1982), pp. 24–35, reference at p. 24.

21 See Allan Wolter's selection of translations: *Duns Scotus on the Will and Morality* (Washington DC: Catholic University of America Press, 1986), pp. 178–205, esp. p. 183.

22 Three distinct views of human freedom be gleaned from Scotus, represented by the work of (1) Lawrence Roberts, "John Duns Scotus and the Concept of Human Freedom," in *Deus et Homo ad mentem I. Duns Scotus* (Romae: Societas Internationalis Scotistica, 1972), pp. 317–325; (2) Douglas Langston, *God's Willing Knowledge* (University Park, PA: Pennsylvania State University Press, 1986); and (3) William Frank, "Duns Scotus' Concept of Willing Freely: What Divine Freedom beyond Choice Teaches Us," *Franciscan Studies* 42 (1982), 68–89.

23 The illuminating and irenic article by Patrick Lee, "The Relation between Intellect and Will in Free Choice according to Aquinas and Scotus," *Thomist* 49 (1985), 321–340, concludes with these words. His laudable intent to reduce caricature and polarization need not extend, however, to asserting that "they agree on how intellect and will are related in the act of choice" (p. 340), as Joseph Incandela's article ("Duns Scotus and the Experience of Human Freedom," *Thomist* 56 (1992), 229–256) demonstrates: what is intrinsic and constitutive for Aquinas is extrinsic or (at best) coordinate for Scotus (Lee, "Relation between Intellect and Will," pp. 322–326).

24 I am indebted to Joseph Incandela for this observation. On the condemnations of 1277, see Roland Hissette, *Enquête sur les 219 articles condamnés à Paris le 7 mars 1277* (Louvain: Publications Universitaires, 1977).

25 Lee, "Relation between Intellect and Will," p. 341.

26 William Frank, "Duns Scotus on Autonomous Freedom and Divine Co-causality," *Medieval Philosophy and Theology* 2 (1992), 142–164.

27 Lee, "Relation between Intellect and Will," pp. 322–326, citing C. Balic, "Une question inédite de J. Duns Scot sur la volonté," *Récherches de Thologie Ancienne et Mediévale* 3 (1931), 191–208, at p. 203; see Frank, "Duns Scotus," where "co-causality" is distinguished from instrumentality.

28 On this propensity and ways to counter it, see Kathryn Tanner, *God and Creation in Christian Theology* (Oxford: Basil Blackwell, 1988).

29 For a sustained analysis of Dante's scheme, see Christian Moevs, *Metaphysics of Dante's Comedy* (Oxford: Oxford University Press, 2005).

30 Herbert Fingarette details the paradoxical features of this pervasive human activity in his *Self-Deception* (New York: Humanities Press, 1969).

31 For a fascinating corroboration of human freedom as "interested, contextualized freedom" see M. Jamie Ferreira, *Transforming Vision: Imagination and Will in Kierkegaardian Faith* (Oxford: Clarendon, 1991), chs 1–3; as well as her study of parallels with Newman in "Leaps and Circles: Kierkegaard and Newman on Faith and Reason," *Religious Studies* 30 (1994), 379–397, esp. p. 390.

32 One may read John Paul's *Veritatis Splendor (The Splendor of Truth)* (Washington, DC: United States Catholic Conference, 1993) as presenting the ethical life in this way.

33 John Milbank, *Theology and Social Theory* (Oxford: Basil Blackwell, 1990). See my review article in *Modern Theology* 8 (1992), 319–330, an issue devoted to responses to Milbank's formidable book.

3

Human Initiative and Divine Grace: Augustine and Ghazali

The strategies developed in the preceding chapter to align free agency of human beings with that of the creator will need to be refined still more to help illuminate the ways a free creator interacts with intentional creatures, so as to intensify the founding and sustaining relation which is the creature's very existing, transforming it into a relationship which can best be described as "interpersonal." Variously called "covenant" by Jews, "grace" by Christians, and "proximity to God" by Muslims, each tradition tries to articulate the way the creator elaborates original creating into a more intentional relating, with telling similarities and differences. There can be no doubt about the reality of human action in each of these traditions, for each is predicated on a human response to a divine invitation. Yet we encounter a recurring question regarding human initiative: does it originate in the subject alone, as it were, or does it rather emerge as response to an invitation, whether primordial or concurrent, or both? In other words, is what we spontaneously identify as initiative better delineated as a response? More radically,

Towards a Jewish-Christian-Muslim Theology, First Edition. David B. Burrell.
© 2011 John Wiley & Sons Ltd. Published 2011 by John Wiley & Sons Ltd.

can there be such a thing as human initiative *tout court*, without its being a response to an offer?

I contend that each of the Abrahamic traditions must say "no," since most radically, each of us is called forth into existence; no one could even exist "on their own." So metaphysically, if you will, human initiative can only take place within a context which reminds us of our dependence on a creator. Yet we remain mostly oblivious of this fact; we even try to create our own context as much as we are able to, so allowing us to act outside of the overarching invitation into being. Yet these too are actions, so we can initiate "on our own," as it were, though these actions will invariably be destructive. William Chittick, a Muslim philosophical theologian, identifies this interweaving of the metaphysical with the ethical with the twin imperatives of Ibn 'Arabi: the moral and the ontological: "God said 'be' and it is" (Q 2:117, 3:47, 6:73). While Nietzsche reminded us how morality depends intrinsically on a creator, aligning the two "imperatives" constitutes the principal challenge to believers, in practice as well as conceptually, for our lived context regularly fails to remind us how we depend on a creator. But we will have room to try to articulate that alignment only when we have moved beyond Nietzsche's presumption: that the presence of a creator cannot but overwhelm human initiative and responsibility. So once again, we are returned to the task of properly articulating the creator/creature relationship, which Chittick identifies as the first or "ontological imperative."

One could argue that the Jewish tradition is able to meld divine and human action more effectively, thanks to the covenant. Christians are invited by Paul to see themselves as "grafted onto the trunk of Israel" (see Rom. 11:17), so participating in the original covenant initiated by the Lord of heaven and earth with the people Israel. The Qur'an also speaks of a primordial covenant which sets the stage for its own advent and the specific invitation it offers, yet that action – with our response – remains in the background in the subsequent tradition, more presupposed than operative. The Hebrew covenant assures that whoever enters into it will always be faced with, contending with, this God who singles out, elects, and calls his own to accounting. Think of Job, whose feisty interaction with the very One who bestows the covenant constitutes an eloquent challenge to those tired spokesmen who have adopted a set way of interpreting (and so attenuating) it. In fact, that would appear to be the very point that the presence of this text in the Jewish canon expresses.[1] Whatever be the reason, the Jewish tradition invariably trumps the other two when it comes to dramatizing the interaction of creator and creatures, notably human creatures. The patriarchs regularly contend with the Lord, in a way which (for example) Jacob would never think of doing in the Qur'anic chapter on Joseph. We may express this difference by noting how Jewish "atheists" are always contending with the God they deny. The covenant seems to have established the presence of God even (and perhaps especially) when that God is absent.

What marks the Jewish tradition is an untrammeled insistence on human beings' free response – whether negative or positive – to the gift of Torah, which already comprises a divine invitation to respond. The Bible enshrines flesh-and-blood stories of the qualities of response, including refusal, which shape the living tradition, so inviting each successive generation to continue shaping it by their response in turn. Yet this One who covenants a people is the very One who constitutes them to be free "in the beginning" so that more philosophical discussions of human freedom in relation to divine freedom are already directed by the very structure of Israelite religion enshrined in biblical narrative. So the creator's constitution as well as commerce with that portion of creation which carries the divine image will always respect the freedom of response inscribed in the individuals who constitute it. No wonder Moses Maimonides found no dissenting voices in Judaism for the contention "that man should have the ability to do whatever he wills or chooses among the things concerning which he has the ability to act" (*Guide* 3.17).[2] Other classical Jewish philosophers will both presume and defend human freedom as well, even when the conceptual formulations they adopted may have veered towards subtle forms of determinism, for biblical structures prevailed.[3]

As a result, Jewish thinkers seldom anguished over the mode of interaction between creator and creatures which preoccupied both Islam and Christianity. They seemed often to be content with Isa. 55:9: "'as far as the heavens are above the earth, so far are my ways above your ways', says the Lord." For it seemed pointless to try to scrutinize the ways of God, whose wisdom in creating left human beings free to respond to the invitations that same God would also freely offer. Indeed, the original gift of covenant assures us that this creator would always leave room for human beings to respond freely. What seemed to force Christianity and Islam to probe more intimately into the interface between the free actions of creator and of creatures was a realization that human beings needed to be divinely assisted to respond freely to God's invitation actively and intimately. Christian reflection names this specific divine activity elevating human beings to intercourse with God, "grace," distinguishing that activity which establishes a standing platform from which to act, "habitual grace," from the activity enhancing discrete acts, "operating grace." This dimension seems to have entered Christian reflection to express the way Paul describes followers of Jesus being incorporated into the original covenant by the "Holy Spirit given to us, pouring into our hearts the love of God" (Rom. 5:5). In Islam, a complementary picture emerges of believers being drawn ever closer to the source of their very existence in an intentional way articulated in "stages" of proximity to God. So Jewish thinkers would in turn appropriate new patterns for expressing human beings' ongoing relation to God, as Georges Vajda elucidates in his magisterial *L'amour de Dieu dans la théologie juine du moyen age* (1957). Together with Marie-Louise Siauve's *L'amour de Dieu chez Ghazali* (1986), these careful and enlightening studies show how both Jewish and Muslim traditions offer distinctive ways of elucidating the relation of creator to intentional creatures on the model of love and of friendship.[4] So let us explore how each tradition will use *love* and *friendship* to model the "interpersonal" relation of creator with intentional creatures.

Engaging both rabbinic and medieval authorities, Vajda centers Jewish reflection on these matters on the way Deuteronomy articulates both "the love God has for Israel, manifested in the gratuity of election, and the love elicited thereby from Israel for God" (p. 17). So Moses: "if [the Lord] set his heart on you and chose you ... it was for the love of you; ... you are therefore to keep and observe the commandments ... that I lay down for you today" (Deut. 7:7, 8, 11). Hosea portrays divine initiative as one of passionate love, echoed in the Lord's promise through Jeremiah: "I have loved you with an everlasting love, so I am constant in my affection for you" (Jer. 31:3). While Jeremiah proceeds to remind us how God's constancy will ever be rewarded by Israel's inconstancy, God's initiative has already set the pattern for the people's response. Jewish liturgy will continue to stress the intimate connection of "the election and love for Israel, with obedience to the commandments the privileged path taken by Israel in its love for God" (p. 33). Later tradition, exemplified by Maimonides, does not hesitate to speak of this love as passionate [*ishq*]: "an excess of love, so that no thought remains that is directed towards anything other than the Beloved" (*Guide* 3.51). We expect Maimonides to elaborate this intercourse in intellectual terms, via "the bond between us and Him, that intellect which overflows from Him" to inform our life and action, so that "those who have obtained this overflow ... can never be afflicted with evil of any kind, for they are with God and God with them" (*Guide* 3.51). And if "philosophy" can effect this union for the learned, observance of the Torah does it for the rest, leading them to "love through the opinions [it teaches], while fear is achieved by means of all the actions prescribed" (*Guide* 3.52). In these final chapters of the *Guide* Maimonides offers a more inclusive picture of the divine-human relation than the starkly intellectual one which is usually attributed to him, rendering the economy of salvation in strict conformity with that of creation, followed by subsequent Jewish tradition.

A recent declaration by more than 300 Muslim signatories – *A Common Word between Us* (2007) – grounding Islam in love of God and neighbor finds palpable support in Muslim tradition, in Ibn Taymiyya as well as al-Ghazali.[5] Explaining why the Qur'an distinguishes "love" from "willing" in God, Ibn Taymiyya suggests that while God wills everything, love is reserved for the inscrutable wisdom of God's "wise purpose [*hikma*]" whereby evil may serve good, which human beings may sometimes discern. All this stems from the gratuity of creation, which "cannot be considered a response to a need existing in God; it is rather a natural and logical working out of the implications of the divine attributers, particularly the attributes of love." So the human response to so altruistic a love must be as selfless as possible, loving God not "for his act of kindness but only, or at least primarily, for himself."[6] More amply, in translating Ghazali's *Kitâb al-Hubb* (*Book of Love*) from the *Ihya' Ulum ad-Din* and offering an extensive commentary in her *L'amour de Dieu chez Ghazali*, Marie-Louise Siauve elaborates how his entire philosophy is structured on a loving relationship between creator and human creatures. Since God creates when there is no reason to do so, the very being of creatures seeks to return the love whereby they originate, and the "infinity of this desire reveals ... the infinity of God".[7] On these metaphysical grounds, Ghazali argues for the suitability of using "passionate love" (*ishq*) for this intercourse between creator and creatures, so long as we recognize that "language uses them in a figurative way to describe the reality of the creator".[8] So the affinity required for interchange between creator and creature, obtains without palpable resemblance (which is the Qur'an's concern). Ibn 'Arabi will carry this exchange one step further, as we shall see, but Ghazali clears the way for Muslims to speak of God's faithful servants being transformed by an intentional union of knowing and loving.

Christianity, of course, resonates with love, insisting that "God is love" (1 Jn 4:16), seeing the person and actions of Jesus as completing the promises made to Jeremiah: "I will make a new covenant with the house of Israel" (31:31). Indeed, Thomas Aquinas will identify the new covenant with "the grace of the Holy Spirit, given to those who believe in Christ."[9] For Jesus bestowed on his disciples the title which the Hebrew Scriptures had reserved for Moses or Abraham, and the Qur'an for Abraham: "I shall not call you servants any more; I call you friends" (Jn 15:15). Now the entire atmosphere of the New Testament breathes the fact that the love which the creator has for creatures is made efficacious for all human beings in Jesus, the Word of God made human. Something new has entered a creation that has been groaning in one great act of giving birth (Rom. 8:23), yet the new is a renewal of the original, for the Word of God who re-creates is the one through whom the One creates. Yet Aquinas will remind us how the new sheds light on the original as well: "the fact that God made all things by His Word excludes the error of those who say God produced things by necessity" (ST 1.32.1.3). And we have seen how both Jewish and Muslim traditions shared this same avowal of a free creation from their respective scriptures.

Yet beyond insisting that the relation of creator to creatures is utterly free – indeed gratuitous, since nothing could impel God to create – how can we address the endemic human propensity to regard it competitively? However odd it may seem, discussions of divine and human freedom often proceed adversarially, as if the freedom of one must stand over against the other. I suggest that "divine vs. human" freedom is odd on the face of it, once we reflect on the relation the act of creating introduces, and how utterly unique it must be. What results – a creature – can hardly be over against its creator as two creatures are inevitably over against each other. Robert Sokolowski employs a phenomenological "conceit" – "the distinction" – to name this ineffable relation, while Kathryn Tanner dubs it "non-contrastive."[10] Another thinker, an English member of the Society of the Sacred Heart, animating an ashram in India for some decades, Sara Grant, adopts Shankara's key term, "non-duality," to name the relation at once connecting as well as distinguishing creatures from the creator. Her Teape lectures, reissued by Bradley Malkovsky, *Towards and Alternative Theology: Confessions of a Non-dualist Christian*, put it this way:[11]

> In India as in Greece, the ultimate question must always be that of the relation between the supreme unchanging Reality and the world of coming-to-be and passing away, the eternal Self and what appears as non-Self, and no epistemology can stand secure as long as this question remains unanswered. [It is indeed this startling contention

which this essay has been exploring.] ... A systematic study of Sankara's use of relational terms made it quite clear to me that he agrees with St. Thomas Aquinas in regarding the relation between creation and the ultimate Source of all being as a *non-reciprocal dependence relation*; i.e., a relation in which subsistent effect or "relative absolute" is *dependent on its cause for its very existence as a subsistent entity*, whereas the cause is *in no way dependent on the effect for its subsistence*, though there is a *necessary logical relation between cause and effect*; i.e., a relation which is *perceived by the mind* when it reflects on the implications of the existence of the cosmos.

Her final observation about a "necessary logical relation" is quite compatible with regarding creating as a free action of the creator, for its import is intended to capture Aquinas's identification of "creation in the creature [as] nothing other than a relation of sorts to the creator as the principle of its existing" (ST 1.45.3).

So the very existence (*esse*) of a creature is an *esse-ad*, an existing which is itself a relation to its source. As we have noted, nothing could better express the way in which Aquinas's formulation of the essence/existing distinction transforms Aristotle than to point out that what for Aristotle "exists in itself" (substance) is for Aquinas derived from an Other in its very in-itselfness, or substantiality. Yet since the Other is the cause of being, each thing which exists-to the creator also exists in itself: derived existence is no less substantial when it is derived from the One-who-is, so it would appear that one could succeed in talking of existing things without explicitly referring them to their source. "The distinction," in other words, need not *appear*. But that simply reminds us how unique a non-reciprocal relation of dependence must be: it characterizes one relation only, that of creatures to creator.

If creator and creature were distinct from each other in an ordinary way, the relation – even one of dependence – could hardly be non-reciprocal, for the fact that something depends from an originating agent, as a child from a parent, must mark a difference in that agent itself. Yet the fact that a cause of being, properly speaking, is not affected by causing all-that-is does not imply remoteness or uncaring; indeed, quite the opposite. For such a One must cause in such a way as to be present in each creature as that to which it is oriented in its very existing. In that sense, this One cannot be considered as *other* than what it creates, in an ordinary sense of that term; just as the creature's *esse-ad* assures that it cannot *be* separately from its source. So it will not work simply to contrast creation to emanation, or to picture the creator distinct (in the ordinary sense) from creation by contrast with a more pantheistic image. Indeed, it is to avoid such infelicities of imagination that Sara Grant has recourse to Sankara's sophisticated notion of "non-duality" to call our attention in an arresting way to the utter uniqueness of "the distinction" which must indeed hold between creator and creation, but cannot be pictured in a contrastive manner.[12]

Nor does Aquinas feel any compunction at defining creation as the "emanation of all of being from its universal cause (*emanatio totius entis a cause universali*)" (ST 1.45.1). Indeed, once he had emptied the emanation scheme of any mediating role, he could find no better way of marking the uniqueness of the causal relation of creation than using the term "emanation" to articulate it.[13] For once the scheme has been gutted, that *sui generis* descriptor should serve to divert us from imaging the creator over-against the universe, as an entity exercising causal efficacy on anything-that-is in a manner parallel to causation within the universe. While the all-important "distinction" preserves God's freedom in creating, which the emanation scheme invariably finesses, we will have learned to be wary of picturing that distinction in a fashion which assimilates the creator to another item within the universe. Harm Goris has shown how close attention to the uniqueness of the creator/creature relation, with its attendant corollary of participation as a way of articulating this *sui generis* causal relation, can neutralize many of the conundra which so fascinate philosophers of religion.[14] Yet that very fascination can also reveal how little explicit reflection on this relation grounding the universe as well as any responsible discourse about its creator can be found in standard "philosophy of religion." Perhaps more robust interfaith inquiry into creation *ex nihilo* will help to show that lacuna for what it is, and help to set philosophers of religion on a more promising trajectory.[15]

Yet experience shows how easily God can be misconstrued as the "biggest thing around," that practitioners of philosophical theology find themselves ever combating idolatry, as Nicholas Lash reminds us.[16] Yet the tone of his remarks is always self-instructing, as if to reveal what a struggle it is for even a seasoned practitioner to execute it properly. We are reminded of Aquinas's prescient remark that we can *at best* "imperfectly signify divinity" (1.13.4), which means, of course, that we will get it wrong most of the time! So something more than brightness or cleverness has to characterize inquirers into these arcane regions.

Notes

1   See my *Deconstructing Theodicy: A Philosophical Commentary on Job* (Grand Rapids, MI: Brazos, 2008).

2   Moses Maimonides, *Guide of the Perplexed* (trans. A.H. Freidlander; New York: Dover, 1956), Bk. 3, Ch. 17.

3   David B. Burrell, *Freedom and Creation in Three Traditions* (Notre Dame, IN: University of Notre Dame Press, 1993).

4   Georges Vajda, *L'amour de Dieu dans la théologie juine du moyen age* (Paris: Vrin, 1957); Marie-Louise Siauve, *L'amour de Dieu chez Ghazali* (Paris: Vrin, 1986). Vajda, like Alexander Altman, is one of those rare writers whose every composition seems to illuminate. Siauve completed her doctorate, including a translation of al-Ghazali's *Kìbâb al-Hubb* (*Book of Love*) from the *Ihya' Ulum ad-Din* (*Livre de l'amour* (Paris: Vrin, 1986)), with Roger Arnaldez, while teaching in a women's lycée in Oran, in a response to alter Algerians' view of the French.

5   See the Common Word website: www.acommonword.com/.

6   See Joseph Norment Bell, *Love Theory in Later Hanbalite Islam* (Albany, NY: State University of New York Press, 1979), pp. 70, 73.

7   Siauve, *L'amour de Dieu chez Ghazali*, p. 294.

8   Siauve, *Livre de l'amour*, pp. 153–154.

9   *Summa Theologiae* (ST) 1-2.106.1.

10 Robert Sokolowski, *God of Faith and Reason* (Washington, DC: Catholic University of America Press, 1995); Kathryn Tanner, *God and Creation in Christian Theology* (Oxford: Basil Blackwell, 1988).

11 Bradley Malkovsky, *Towards an Alternative Theology: Confessions of a Non-dualist Christian* (Notre Dame, IN: University of Notre Dame Press, 2001).

12 Kathryn Tanner develops a sense of transcendence that is expressly "non-contrastive," illustrating that suggestive category though the history of some key questions in philosophical theology, in her *God and Creation in Christian Theology*.

13 See my *Knowing the Unknowable God* (Notre Dame, IN: University of Notre Dame Press, 1987), pp. 86–91.

14 Harm Goris, *Free Creatures of an Eternal God* (Leuven: Peeters, 1996).

15 See Carlo Cogliati, David Burrell, Janet Soskice, and William Stoeger (eds), *Creation and the God of Abraham* (Cambridge: Cambridge University Press, 2010). The presentation of Sara Grant included here has been taken from the conclusion of my contribution to this volume.

16 Nicholas Lash's recent *Theology for Pilgrims* (Notre Dame, IN: University of Notre Dame Press, 2008) deftly exhibits the quality of dialectical reasoning which must attend reliable judgment in "matters divine."

4

Trust in Divine Providence: *Tawakkul*, "Abandonment," and "Detachment"

We have seen how philosophical accounts attempting to relate human to divine freedom – or more properly, created to uncreated free action – offer a richly contested archive. Yet such discussions remain on the periphery of the religious lives of Jews, Christians, and Muslims, and in their contemporary mode often import presumptions regarding human freedom which are at variance with a longer and richer tradition, and can easily skew the best renditions of free action operative in the traditions we are canvassing, doing so in quest of a chimera called "autonomy." This chapter rather attempts a coherent account of ways in which authentically free creatures cannot fail to be dependent on their creator. To do so we shall venture into the heart of life in the spirit, comparing and contrasting two key works in Christianity and Islam: Jean-Pierre de Caussade's *L'Abandon à la Providence divine* (1741), recently translated into English afresh as *The Sacrament of the Present Moment* (1982); and Abu Hamid al-Ghazali's (d. 1111) *Kitab al-tawhid wa tawakkul* (Bk 35 of his *Ihya' Ulum ad-Din*), translated as *Faith in Divine*

Towards a Jewish-Christian-Muslim Theology, First Edition. David B. Burrell.
© 2011 John Wiley & Sons Ltd. Published 2011 by John Wiley & Sons Ltd.

Unity and Trust in Divine Providence (2000).[1] Classical Jewish figures commenting on the quality of trust elicited by the divine bestowal of covenant on the people Israel will facilitate the comparison and offer contrast at key points. By introducing authors central to each tradition in this fashion, so we should be able to deconstruct stereotypes each might have of the other. It will also become evident how much illuminating presumes paths to understanding in each tradition presume a robust free creation, respecting the "distinction" of creator from creatures so that one is never pitted against the other, as though we were in the presence of two competitive individuals.

Let us begin with al-Ghazali, whose death in 1111 gives him evident priority. And while there was clearly no exchange between him and de Caussade, it will not be difficult to display a profound affinity of one for the other. Again, daily practice suggests this comparison, given the ubiquity of "al-hamd il-Allah" – "God be praised" – throughout the Muslim world. Christians may quite readily attach this expletive to good fortune, but would be less inclined to let it fall in the face of affliction; whereas my Muslims friends in Gaza, in the midst of interminable siege, would invariably respond in this way. Their witness has taught me that it should be as appropriate to the reception of bad news as of good. Yet proposing that can be unnerving for Western Christians, however much they might be exhorted to "trust in God." They would be far more prone to resist such even-handedness, attributing the practice to "Islamic fatalism" – the stereotype ready to hand. But let us inquire how a noted Muslim theologian, al-Ghazali, approaches trusting in divine providence, linking it intimately with our existential ties to a free creator.

Al-Ghazali: Trust Emanating from Faith in One God[2]

His book entitled *Faith in Divine Unity and Trust in Divine Providence* (*Kitab al-tawhid wa'l-tawakkul*) of the *Ihya' 'Ulum al-Din* (*Revivifying Religious Sciences*) eminently qualifies al-Ghazali as a Muslim theologian in the full medieval meaning of that term, and not merely in the descriptive sense extended to include any thinker adept at *kalam,* or the dialectical defense of faith. For Ghazali was never content to use human reason as he found it elaborated in Ibn Sina and others, merely to defend the faith but rather employed it to lead Muslim faithful to a deeper penetration of the mysteries of their revealed religion, the central of which is the free creation of the universe by the one God. The works of the philosophers themselves were not always helpful to him in their native state, so he set out first to purify them of their pretensions to offer an access to truth independent of and superior to that of divine revelation-the Qur'an. Hence his need to understand them thoroughly, embodied in the work entitled *The Intentions of the Philosophers* (*Maqasid al-falasifa*), itself conceived as an extended introduction (and hence also published as the *Muqaddima al-Tahafut*) to his *Deconstruction of the Philosophers* (*Tahafut al-falasifa*).[3] The negative tone of this latter work, together with its detailed refutation by Averroes Ibn Rushd: *Tahafut al-Tahafut,* has left the impression that Ghazali should never be ranked with "the philosophers" but always left with "the theologians" as a defender of *kalam* orthodoxy in the face of reasonable inquiry. It is precisely that stereotype which this book challenges, and so can offer Ghazali's own assistance to deconstruct the historical image which he helped to create for himself.

The *Book of Faith in Divine Unity (tawhid) and Trust in Divine Providence (tawakkul)* is Book 35 in Ghazali's masterwork, the *Ihya' 'Ulum al-Din.* The French summary of this *magnum opus,* entitled *Revivification des sciences religieuses,* reminds us how forceful is the key term taken from the fourth form of the Arabic verb (*ihya*), probably best rendered in English as "Putting Life Back into Religious Learning."[4] For that would convey Ghazali's intent, as well as his assessment of the state of such learning in his time. He is intent upon a lucid understanding of matters religious, yet one which continues to give primacy to practice: faith is rooted in trust and so needs be expressed in a life of trust. The pretensions of the philosophers to understand the mysteries of *the heavens and the earth and all that is between them* (Q 15:85), proceeding by conceptual argument alone, must be exposed as just that – pretension – in the face of the assertion so central to Muslim faith: that the universe was *freely* created by the one sovereign God. Yet human reason will prove an indispensable tool to direct our minds and our hearts to understand how to think and how to live as a consequence of that signal truth.

Such is Ghazali's intent. It is displayed in the structure of his *Ihya'* as well as in the pattern adopted for his treatise expounding the 99 canonical "names" of God, where he devotes an extensive introduction to explaining the human practice of naming and how it might be understood in relation to the names which God has given Himself in the Qur'an.[5] It turns out that the only way to extend the limits of human knowledge of such divine things is by "adorning oneself" with the meaning of the names, so the commentary on each name begins with semantics and closes with a counsel: how one might oneself become more like God so presented. This pattern will become the master strategy of the *Ihya'* as well, where the entire gamut of Muslim life – beliefs together with practices – is laid out in a way which displays the importance of both *knowledge* and *state* (of being), that is, of understanding together with practice. Readers familiar with Aquinas will marvel at the way in which Ghazali's master plan aligns with that thinker's insistence that theology is at once a speculative and a practical mode of knowing.[6]

It is fair to say that the *Kitab al-Tawhid wa' l-Tawakkul* plays an axial role among the other books in the *Ihya'*. For *tawhid,* or "faith in divine unity," sounds the distinctive note of Islam which grounds everything Muslims believe in the *shahada:* "There is no god but God." Islamic reflection on *tawhid is* reminiscent of rabbinic commentary on divine unity as evidenced in the *shema:* "Hear, O Israel, the Lord our God, the Lord is One" (Deut. 6:4). It is hardly at issue that God be one rather than many; it rather points directly to the injunction against idolatry: all Israelites know thereby that they must orient their entire lives to God – through the Torah, to be sure – and nowhere else. So a philosophical argument culminating in the assertion that God is one would hardly interest the rabbis, nor would it Ghazali. Its conclusion may be true enough, but what is at issue is not the unity itself, but the implications of the community's *faith* in divine unity. Yet that cannot be a blind faith, so what is being asserted? That everything comes from God and that "there is no agent but God."

In assessing degrees of assent to this *shahada*, Ghazali notes:

> The third kind [of believer] professes faith in divine unity in the sense that he sees but a single agent, since truth is revealed to him as it is in itself; and he only sees in reality a single agent, since reality has revealed itself to him as it is in itself because he has set his heart on determining to comprehend the word "reality" [*haqiqa*], and this stage belongs to lay folk as well as theologians. (p. 11)

He sketches out the two-part structure of the book by way of showing how *tawakkul* – trust in divine providence – is grounded in an articulate *tawhid*, as practice is anchored in faith, or *state* [of being] in *knowledge*. In doing so, he is even more insistent: this first part

> will consist in showing you that there is no agent but God the Most High: of all that exists in creation: sustenance given or withheld, life or death, riches or poverty, and everything else that can be named, the sole one who initiated and originated it all is God Most High. And when this has been made clear to you, you will not see anything else, so that your fear will be of Him, your hope in Him, your trust in Him, and your security with Him, for He is the sole agent without any other. Everything else is in His service, for not even the smallest atom in the worlds of heaven and earth is independent of Him for its movement. If the gates of mystical insight were opened to you, this would be clear to you with a clarity more perfect than ordinary vision (pp. 15–16).

These last words are telling, and signal Ghazali's "method" in the first section elaborating faith in divine unity. There is no attempt to show *how* everything-that-is emanates from the creator; that would be beyond the capacity of our intellect to grasp. And should we try, we would invariably end up articulating something like Ibn Sina's emanation scheme, modeled on logical inference so amounting to a twin denial of divine and of human freedom.[7] Indeed, when

Ghazali tries to articulate what he attributes to mystical insight, it sounds uncannily like Ibn Sina, though he begins with a characteristic verse from the Qur'an: *"we did not create heaven and earth and what lies between them in jest; we did not create them but in truth"* (44:38–39):

> Now all that is between heaven and earth comes forth in a necessary order that is true and consequent, and it is inconceivable that it be otherwise than the way it comes forth, according to this order which exists. For a consequent only follows because it awaits its condition; for a conditioned before a condition would be absurd, and absurdity cannot be ascribed to the being of an object of divine omnipotence. So knowledge [can be said to] follow upon sperm only if one supplies the condition of a living thing, and the will which comes after knowledge [can be said to] follow upon sperm only if the condition of knowledge be supplied as well. All of this offers a way of necessity and the order of truth. There is no room for play or chance in any of this; everything has its rationale and order. Understanding this is difficult … (p. 40).

So he will offer images to move us away from a literal acceptance of the Avicenna-like scheme, for in such matters human reason can at best offer models; yet neither mode of apperception is privileged for Ghazali, in contrast to "the philosophers," notably Averroes.[8] The images offered by the Qur'an, however, will certainly take precedence.

But what about human freedom? Have we not exalted God's sovereign freedom, as the only agent there is, to the inevitable detriment of human initiative? It certainly appears that the intent of Ghazali's images is to take us by the hand and lead us on, in hopes that we

> may come to understand the emanation of things so ordained [*muqaddarat*] from the eternal omnipotence, even though the omnipotent One is eternal and the things ordained [*mqgdurat*] temporal. But this [train of thought] knocks on another door, to another world of the worlds of unveiling. So let us leave all that, since our aim is to

offer counsel regarding the way to faith in divine unity in practice: that the true agent is One, that He is the subject of our fear and our hope, and the One in whom we trust and depend. (pp. 41–42)

These gnomic words will be somewhat clarified in the text itself, but he also wants to show us that the test of our understanding of divine unity will not come by way of clever philosophical schemes but through a life of trust (*tawakkul*), in which concerted practice will bring each of us personally to the threshold of the only understanding possible here, that of "unveiling."[9] Yet some clarifications can be made; reason can offer some therapeutic hints to attenuate the apparent scandal.

He introduces a typically Muslim objection:

How can there be any common ground between faith in divine unity and the *sharia* [religious law]? For the meaning of faith in divine unity is that there is no god but God Most High, and the meaning of the law lies in establishing the actions proper to human beings [as servants of God]. And if human beings are agents, how is it that God Most High is an agent? Or if God Most High is an agent, how is a human being an agent? There is no way of understanding "acting" as between these two agents. In response, I would say: indeed, there can be no understanding when there is but one meaning for "agent." But if it had two meanings, then the term comprehended could be attributed to each of them without contradiction, as when it is said that the emir killed some-one, and also said that the executioner killed him; in one sense, the emir is the killer and in another sense, the executioner. Similarly, a human being is an agent in one sense, and God – Great and Glorious – is an agent in another. The sense in which God Most High is agent is that He is the originator[10] of existing things [*al-mukhtari' al-mawjud*], while the sense in which a human being is an agent is that he is the locus [*mahal*] in which power is created after will has been created, and that after knowledge had been created, so that power depends on will, and movement is linked to power, as a conditioned to its condition. But depending on the power of God is like the dependence of effect on cause, and of the originated on the originator. So every thing which depends on a power in such a way as it is the locus of the power is called "agent"

in a manner which expresses that fact of its dependence, much as the
executioner can be called "killer" and the emir a killer, since the
killing depends on the power of both of them, yet in different respects.
In that way both of them are called "killer", and similarly, the things
ordained [*maqrurat*] depend on two powers. (p. 43)

He goes on to note how the Qur'an often attributes agency both
to God and to creatures, showing that revelation acknowledges and
exploits the inherently analogous character of *agency* as exhibited
in the multiple uses of the term "agent." This small clue offers us
the best way of presenting Ghazali's intent and his strategy to contemporary readers. What he wanted to do was to help believers to
recognize that theirs is a unique perspective on the universe: each
thing is related in its very existence to the one from whom it freely
comes. (As Aquinas will put it: "the very existence of creatures is
to-be-related to their creator" (ST 1.45.3).) Yet since we cannot articulate this founding and sustaining relationship conceptually, for to
do so would trespass on divine freedom, we can only display our
understanding by the way we live our life: trusting in the One who
so sustains us.

To the recurring objection that all this amounts to *jabr* (coercion)
on the part of God, he replies:

This has to do with the divine decree [*qadar*],[11] intimations of which
we saw with respect to the faith in divine unity which brings about
the state of trust in divine providence, and is only perfected by faith
in the benevolence and wisdom [of God]. And if faith in divine unity
brings about insight into the effects of causes, abundant faith in
benevolence is what brings about confidence in the effects of the
causes, and the state of trust in divine providence will only be perfected, as I shall relate, by confidence in the trustworthy One [*wakil*]
and tranquility of heart towards the benevolent oversight of the
[divine] sponsor. For this faith is indeed an exalted chapter in the
chapters of faith, and the stories about it from the path of those experiencing the unveiling go on at length. ... He enhanced knowledge,
wisdom, and reason in a great number of [Sufi sheikhs], and then
unveiled for them the effects of things [*al-'awaqil al-amur*], apprising

them of the secrets of the intelligible world, teaching them the subtleties of speech and the hidden springs of punishment, to the point where they were thus informed regarding what is good or evil, useful or harmful. (pp. 47–48)

This summary offers a springboard to part two of the book, which relates one Sufi story after another, while judiciously selecting them and weaving them into a pattern that allows persons to discriminate in making subtle decisions regarding the way they lead their lives aware of God's benevolent care, exhibiting the sorts of choices they make in typical situations. If Ghazali closes the first part with what looks like a backward-looking conceptual reminder, he opens the way to an entirely different mode of consideration in part two:

Indeed, all this happens according to a necessary and true order, according to what is appropriate as it is appropriate, and in the measure proper to it; nor is anything more fitting, more perfect, and more attractive within the realm of possibility. For if something were to exist and remind one of the sheer omnipotence [of God] and not of the good things accomplished by His action, that would utterly contradict [God's] generosity, and be an injustice contrary to the Just One.[12] And if God were not omnipotent, He would be impotent, thereby contradicting the nature of divinity. (p. 45)

Yet omnipotence cannot be the last word; generosity is a more operative one, for it modifies God's omnipotence in the direction of a benevolent creator. The upshot of *tawhid*, then, must be the believer's profound conviction "of the unalterable justice and excellence of things as they are … of the 'perfect rightness of the actual'."[13]

Eric Ormsby sees this conviction as the upshot of the ten years of seclusion and prayer following Ghazali's spiritual crisis. By "the actual" he means what God has decreed, itself the product and reflection of divine wisdom. And by asserting the primacy of the actual over the possible, Ghazali shows himself a true theologian. Contingency, for philosophers, tends to focus on the logical fact that "whatever exists could always be other than it is." Yet while it may be "logically correct and permissible to affirm that our world could be different than it is, it is not theologically correct and permissible – indeed, it is impious – to assert that our world could be better than it is. The world in all its circumstances remains unimpeachably right and just, and it is unsurpassably excellent."[14] Yet the excellence in question is not one which we can assess independently of the fact that it is the product of divine wisdom, so Ghazali is not asserting that ours is the "best of all possible worlds," as though there were a set of such worlds "each of which might be ranked in terms of some intrinsic excellence." Such an assertion would miss the point of Ghazali's quest: to find ways of expressing that relation of creator to creatures which quite resists formulation. The deconstructive moment had been his rejection of the emanation scheme; the constructive task is taken up in this twin discourse on faith in divine unity and trust in divine providence, but especially in this second part where practice will allow us to traverse domains which speculative reason cannot otherwise map.

What sort of a practice is *tawakkul*: trust in divine providence? It entails accepting whatever happens as part of the inscrutable decree of a just and merciful God. Yet such an action cannot be reduced to mere *resignation*, and so caricatured as "Islamic fatalism." It rather entails aligning oneself with things as they really are: in Ghazali's sense, with the truth that there is no agent but God Most High. This requires effort since we cannot formulate the relationship between this single divine agent and the other agents which we know, and also because our ordinary perspective on things is not a true one: human society lives under the sign of *jahiliyya* or pervasive ignorance. Nor can this effort be solely intellectual; that is, I cannot learn "the truth" in such a way as to align myself with it, in the time-honored fashion in which speculative reason is supposed to illuminate practical judgment. For this all-important relationship resists formulation. Nevertheless, by trying our best to act according to the conviction that the divine decree expresses the truth in events as they unfold, we can allow ourselves to be *shown* how things truly lie. So faith (*tawhid*) and practice (*tawakkul*) are reciprocal; neither is foundational. The understanding we can have is that of one journeying in faith, *a salik,* the name which Sufis characteristically appropriated for themselves.

There are stages of trust in divine providence, to be sure, which Ghazali catalogs as (1) the heart's relying on the trustworthy One (*wakil*) alone, (2) a trust like that of a child in its mother, where the focus is less on the *trust* involved than on the person's orientation to the one in whom they trust; and (3) the notorious likeness of a corpse in the hands of its washers, where the relevant point is that such trust moves one quite beyond petition of any sort (pp. 58–60). Yet the operative factor is present already in the initial stage, which is not surpassed but only deepened by subsequent stages: trusting in the One alone. The formula for faith here is the hadith: "There is no might and power but in God," which Ghazali shows to be equivalent to the Qur'anic *shahadah: There is no god but God,* thereby reminding us that the hadith does not enjoin us to trust in *power* or *might,* as attributes distinct from God, but in God alone. It is in this context that he selects stories of Sufi sheikhs, offering them as examples to help point us towards developing specific skills of trusting: habits of responding to different situations in such a way that one learns by acting how things are truly ordered, the truth of the decree. The principal operative throughout is that a policy of complete renunciation of means (*asbab*) is contrary to divine wisdom, the *sunna Allah,* but those who journey in faith will be cognizant that there are different kinds of means, as they become aware of hidden as well as manifest ones.

The situations which he canvasses begin with the daily question of sustenance: should one seek it by working for it, or ought one wait for it to come to him or her? At issue here is a practice of some Sufis to sequester themselves in a mosque in prayer while relying on the generosity of the faithful, as well as more dramatic adventures of journeying into the desert without provisions. Ghazali notes with approval that when the illustrious al-Hawwas undertook such journeys, he never left home without four items: a pot, a rope, scissors, and a needle and thread. For while he was convinced that God would provide for him on his journey, he realized that, according to the *sunna* of *Allah,* water would not be found on the surface of the desert (hence the pot and the rope), and should his sole tunic rip he would not be likely to run across a tailor (hence the scissors, needle and thread: "lest his nakedness be exposed" (p. 76)). He also notes that judiciousness in such matters will differ considerably whether one be a single person or a householder. Other situations which involve a judicious practice of trust in divine providence include saving, repelling injury or resisting danger, our response to theft of our property, and the manner in which we relate to illness: ought one or may one simply dispense with all treatment? May we conceal the fact that we are ill from those who care for us, or must we disclose it? Here especially he strives for a sane "middle way": dispensing with treatment cannot be said always to be the "better way" for those who trust in God's providence.

The bevy of stories which Ghazali mines offer living examples of the attitude proper to one who firmly believes in divine unity, namely, a total trust in God's providential care. He uses them to offer one object lesson after another of a way to take esoteric Sufi lore and allow it to inspire one's practice, as in the following:

> Should you say that it has been said of certain ones that a lion put his paws on their shoulders without their being agitated, I would respond: It is said about certain ones that they ride lions and make them subservient, but there is no need to deceive yourselves about that station.[15] For even if it were authentic in itself, it would hardly be healthy to imitate a path which one learns about from someone else. That station is marked by an abundance of miracles and is certainly not a condition for trusting in God; it is rather replete with secrets which cannot be divined by those who have not attained it. You might also say: What are the signs by which I could know that I had attained it? I would respond: One who attains it does not need to look for signs. However, one of the signs of that station does in fact precede it: that a dog become subject to you, a dog which is always with you, indeed inside your skin, named Anger [or Resentment]. [Normally] it does not stop biting you and biting others. But if this dog becomes subservient to you, to the extent that when it becomes agitated and irritated it will be subject to you instantaneously, then your standing will be enhanced to the point where a lion,

the *very* king of beasts, will be subject to you. It is more appropriate that the dog in your house be subject to you than a dog in the desert; but it is even more appropriate that the dog inside your skin be subject to you than the dog in your house. For if the dog within is not subject to you, how can you hope to make the dog outside subject to you? (p. 115)

So there is a school whereby we learn how to respond to what happens in such a way that we are shown how things are truly ordered. This school will involve learning from others who are more practiced in responding rightly; Ghazali's judicious use of stories is intended to intimate the Sufi practice of master/disciple wherein the novice is helped to discern how to act. Philosophy is no longer identified as a higher wisdom; speculative reason is wholly subject to practical reason, but that is simply the inevitable implication of replacing the emanation scheme with an intentional creator.[16] So the challenge of understanding the relation of the free creator to the universe becomes the task of rightly responding to events as they happen, in such a way that the true ordering of things, the divine decree, can be made manifest in one's actions-as-responses. Ghazali expresses this relationship between speculative and practical reason by noting that we need to call upon both *knowledge* and *state* (of being) in guiding our actions according to a wholehearted trust in God. What he wishes to convey by those terms in tandem is an awareness of the very structure of the book itself: when put into practice, the *knowledge* which faith in divine unity brings can lead one to a habitual capacity to align one's otherwise errant responses to situation after situation according to that faith. In short, what Ghazali terms *a state*, relying here on a Sufi anthropology, would be more familiar to Western readers as Aristotle's stable "second nature" of virtue.

It is tied, however, not to the Hellenic paradigm of "the magnanimous man" but to a Quranic faith. This is also evident in his treatise on the names of God, for it is the 99 names culled from the Qur'an, names by which God reveals the many "faces" of the divine, which offer a composite picture for human perfection. If we take names to identify attributes, then that book can be read in two distinct, yet related, ways: as a condensed summary of Islamic theology and as offering a revealed counterpart to Aristotle's *Ethics*. Perhaps enough has been said so far to begin to make my case for Ghazali as an Islamic theologian, in the normative and not merely descriptive sense of that term. If he tends to resolve to mystical insight in places where philosophers would prefer conceptual schemes, one ought to acknowledge that he is thereby suggesting that certain domains quite outstrip human conceptualizing. Yet more significant, however, is that everything he says about practice can be carried out quite independently of such "mystical insight," as indeed it must be for the vast majority of faithful.

Jean-Pierre de Caussade: One Abandoning Oneself to Divine Providence

The title of a recent English translation of Jean-Pierre de Caussade's *L'Abandon a la providence divine* (1741) by Kitty Muggeridge, *The Sacrament of the Present Moment* (1982), displays something of the work's metaphysical import, recalling (from Augustine's *Confessions*) how the reality of the present moment both eludes us and furnishes our vital connection with the creator. In this vein, it offers a remarkable parallel to Ghazali's treatise, though in a quite different idiom and context of faith. De Caussade was a Jesuit priest, professor, and spiritual director for Visitation nuns in Nancy from 1729 to 1739. These women transcribed his conferences so as to display something of the verve and intensity with which he delivered them. In the context, he had to distinguish his teaching from a pervading "quietist" ethos which eschewed action in favor of a receptive faith in God's presence and action in the lives of believers. Yet as we shall see, that very strategy suffuses his orienting talks and admonitions to the sisters, so we can only surmise that what distinguished him was the judicious manner in which he approached these delicate issues. Delicate, because they involve interaction between divine and human freedom, so inevitably incorporate one's sense of the ineffable relation between free creator and free creatures. He had taught Greek, Latin, and philosophy before attaining a doctorate in theology at the University of Toulouse in 1708, and served as director of theological students in the Jesuit house in Toulouse for the last five years of his life of 76 years. So the heartfelt and sustained teaching this small book delivers presumes an intellectual infrastructure it seldom reveals, which may also explain how it has endured as a classic of the life of the spirit.

In a comparative spirit, let us note the way Ghazali grounds *tawakkul* in faith:

> If you assert in your soul, either by way of unveiling or by a decisive conviction, that there is no agent but God, as we have insisted; and you are convinced along with that of the perfection of [His] knowledge and power to meet all the needs of human beings, and then of the perfection of [His] solicitude, sympathy and lovingkindness towards human beings as a whole and individually – and that no power surpasses the reach of His power, no knowledge the range of His knowledge, nor does any solicitude of lovingkindness exceed what He has for you – then entrust our heart without hesitation to Him alone, without inclining at all to anything other than Him, nor to one's own self, one's own might or strength. (pp. 55–56)

As we expound de Caussade, this very quality of faith will continually emerge, implicitly and explicitly, in his confident direction, while the constant recurrence of "surrender" cannot but remind one of customary readings of the term "Islam" as "submission."

"Living by faith and the instinct of faith is the same thing. It is joy in God's goodness and trust founded on the hope of his protection; a faith which delights in an accepts everything with good grace" (p. 23). This expresses the leitmotif of de Caussade's guide to living by faith.

> The object of faith [is] to discover God in [the ordinary tasks of life]; to follow and surrender to him is its exercise. ... How otherwise can this divine unity, this spiritual essence, be expressed? How can its nature and meaning be truly conveyed? (pp. 27–28)

That is to say, such perfect trust (or *tawakkul*) can only be grounded in faith in the all-pervasive activity of the one creator (or *tawhid*). Yet as we might expect, de Caussade finds the quality of perfect trust he presents confirming a triune God: "How [otherwise] can the concept of three in one [be] illumined?" (p. 28). Yet what links them both is the claim that a faith which outreaches human understanding, and finding different expression in each case, will be confirmed in an inexhaustible trust:

> To long to be the subject and instrument of divine action and to believe that it operates in each moment and in all things in so far as it finds more or less good will – this is the faith I am preaching. (p. 31)

Yet like the faith itself, the ways God directs believers will defy human calculation:

> He knows, too, that you do not know what is for your good and makes it his business to provide it, little caring whether you like it or not. You are going East, he will turn you to the West. You are set on a fair course, he turns the rudder and sends you back to harbour. Without either compass or map, your voyage is always successful. (p. 34)

Hearers of the Qur'an will be reminded of Moses' celebrated encounter with "the Lord's servant," who kept subverting Moses' plans, only to remind him of the disasters which he would have met in each case, had he prevailed on his original course (18:60–82). Moreover, de Caussade likens those schooled by surrender to such an apparently contrary guide to "a musician who combines long practice with a perfect understanding of music," whose compositions "conformed perfectly to the conventions [yet] he was most successful when working unhampered by them – so much so, that connoisseurs would hail his impromptus as masterpieces" (p. 38). So too with those "acting on intuition and faith in all things: ... all they have to do is to act as though by chance, trusting only to the power of grace which can never be wrong" (p. 39). In short, their mode of acting in consonance with their faith in the presence of their creator, offers a created imitation of the spontaneity of a creator whose wisdom can never be compared to a plan, whose intelligence defies design.

Yet living in this way cannot but defy as well our own conceptions of right and wrong:

> The point must be reached where the whole of creation counts for nothing and God for everything. This is the reason why God opposes all our personal inclinations and ideas. No sooner do we form our own ideas ... or whatever designs we may have or advice we may take, God disconcerts all our plans and instead permits us to find in them only confusion, trouble, vanity and folly. (p. 51)

Yet once freed of the preoccupation of guiding our own life,

> what we do through grace, and what grace accomplishes in us, requires nothing more than surrender or assent. ... It is enough, then, for us to know what we must do, and this is the easiest thing in the world. It is to love God as the mighty all in all, to rejoice in him and to fulfill our duty conscientiously and wisely. (p. 52)

We find here echoes of Ghazali's insistence that "there is no agent but God Most High," as well as his carefully distancing himself from a prevailing "quietism" by knowing what it is for us to do and doing it.

But how to find the secret of "belonging to God" in this way?

> There is none, unless it be to take advantages of every opportunity. Everything leads to union with him; ... only take things as they come without interfering. Everything guides, purifies, and sustains you, carrying you along, so to speak, under God's banner by whose hand earth, air and water are made divine. His power is vaster and more immense than all the elements. ... His Holy Spirit pervades every atom in your body, to the very marrow of your bones (p. 72). ... Without knowing it, all are instruments of that spirit to bring the message freshly to the world (p. 73). ... This is what the book of life

is about. … In it will be written down every thought, word, deed and suffering of all souls. And that scripture will then be a complete record of divine action (p. 74), [a] divine action [which] arranges it all miraculously, [providing] each moment with its appropriate purpose, and the pure of heart, uplifted by faith, find everything good and wish for neither more nor less than what they have. They continually bless that divine hand which pours its living water over them; they treat their friends and enemies alike with the same gentleness, since it was Jesus' way to treat everyone as divine. (p. 87)

Clear references to Jesus and the Holy Spirit are reinforced by biblical imagery of "living water," while the entire thematic echoes Ghazali's insistence that "all this happens according to a necessary and true order, according to what is appropriate as it is appropriate, and in the measure proper to it; nor is anything more fitting, more perfect, and more attractive within the realm of possibility." This conviction is identified by Ormsby: "the world in all its circumstances remains unimpeachably right and just, and it is unsurpassably excellent."[17] This robust faith in a world created freely by the one God is shared by Muslims and Christians, and while revealed differently, each tradition shares those "divine names" which remove the benevolence of this creator-God from all human projection. Yet that conviction and faith need to be confirmed in practice:

The more enlightened, intelligent and capable a person is, the more he is to be feared if he does not have that fundamental goodness which consists in being contented with God and his will. A steadfast heart unites us to divine action. Without it all is purely human nature and usually pure contradiction to God's order, which has not, to tell the truth, any other instruments than the meek (p. 90).

The "steadfast heart" of which de Caussade speaks results from surrender. It is, in fact,

the only secret of surrender, an open secret, an art without artistry. It is the straight path which God requires everyone to follow, explains

very clearly and makes very simple (p. 99). [It involves] going back
to the beginning, the source, the origin of things, where everything
has another name, another shape; where everything is transcenden-
tal, divine, holy, where everything is part of the bounty of Jesus
Christ, where everything is a foundation stone of a heavenly
Jerusalem (pp. 102–103).

This valedictory passage builds on a "surrender" which yields a
"straight path" back to "the beginning" where all is pristine from
the creator. The rich imagery is redolent of both Christian and
Muslim themes, but especially in the way it is anchored in creation
itself, as Elena Malits and I explored in *Original Peace* a decade ago,
showing how early Christian reflection anchored that tradition
securely in free creation, and how everything in Islam turns on that
fulcrum, from the Qur'an's lapidary "God said 'be' and it is" to the
very coming down of that revelation itself.[18]

Moses Maimonides and the Psalmists on Trust

Many find the Hebrew psalms never cease to exalt a crushing
victory of the favored people of God over everyone else, yet they
are also suffused with exhortations to a trust in a forgiving God
which over-reach boundaries of any sort. This is the overriding
reason why Christians share the psalms with Jews as their daily diet
of prayer. A classic summary text can be found in the Septuagint
rendering of Daniel, where a searing self-examination offers a
prelude to a testimonial of trust:

> For your name's sake, O Lord, do not deliver us up forever, or make
> void your covenant. Do not take away your mercy from us, for the
> sake of Abraham, your beloved, Isaac your servant, and Israel your
> holy one, To whom you promised to multiply their offspring like the
> stars of heaven, or the sand on the shore of the sea. For we are reduced,
> O Lord, beyond any other nation, brought low everywhere in the
> world this day because of our sins. We have in our day no prince,
> prophet, or leader, no burnt offering, sacrifice, oblation, or incense,

no place to offer first fruits, to find favor with you. But with contrite heart and humble spirit let us be received. As though it were burnt offerings of rams and bullocks, or thousands of fat lambs, So let our sacrifice be in your presence today as we follow you unreservedly; for those who trust in you cannot be put to shame (Dan. 3:34–43).

This same dynamic is reflected in Solomon Ibn Gabirol's *Kingly Crown*, a staple of the Jewish liturgy, especially for *Yom Kippur*.[19] A native of Andalusia who died in his early thirties (c. 1058), Ibn Gabirol offers testimony a century before the Rambam of the ways "the thought of ancient Greece was to come to Judaism … through the Arabs" (Gluck Preface, 12). His Arabic prose treatise was translated into Latin as *Fons Vitae* [*Source of Life*], which allows him to play a role in medieval philosophy as "Avicebron." Chapter 35 of his long poem, *The Kingly Crown*, reiterates the dual themes of the Septuagint Daniel:

O my God! My face falls when I remember all that I have done to offend Thee; for all the good thou hast vouchsafed to me I have repaid Thee with evil.

For Thou didst create me not of necessity, but as a bounty. Not by compulsion, but by will and love.

Before I was, Thou didst greet me with Thy mercy, breathe spirit into me, and give me life.

And after I came forth into the air of the world, Thou didst not leave me, but like an indulgent father Thou didst cherish me.

As a sucking child didst thou nurse me, and at my mother's breast didst set me securely.

With thy sweet delights Thou didst sate me, and when I came to stand Thou didst strengthen me and set me upright.

Thou didst take me in thine arms and guide me, and teach me wisdom and conduct.

This theme of acknowledging sinfulness is inextricably linked to an original merciful creator, whose caring love endures in the gift of

Torah. This dimension will be elaborated a century later in the *Guide of the Perplexed*. Returning to the Septuagint psalm of Daniel to note how the fruit of trust is not victory over one's enemies but removal of shame, Maimonides will use it to frame his conviction and that those who trust in God can never be harmed:

> if we prepare ourselves, and attain the influence of the Divine Intellect, Providence is joined to us, and we are guarded against all evils. "The Lord is on my side; I will not fear; what can man do unto me"? (Ps. 98:6) "Acquaint now thyself with him, and be at peace" (Job 22:21); i.e., turn unto Him, and you will be safe from all evil. Consider the Psalm on mishaps, and see how the author describes that great Providence, the protection and defense from all mishaps.[20]

And lest Maimonides' reputation for granting unyielding primacy to intellect predispose us to misread these final chapters of the *Guide of the Perplexed*, he focuses on the Torah:

> God declares in plain words that it is the object of all religious acts to produce in man fear of God and obedience to His word – the state of mind which we have demonstrated in this chapter for those who desire to know the truth, as being our duty to seek. ... The two objects, love and fear of God, are acquired by two different means. The love is the result of the truths taught in the Law, including the true knowledge of the Existence of God; whilst fear of God is produced by the practices prescribed in the Law. (3.42).

According to the rabbis, confessing the unicity of God should bear the existential fruit of a unyielding trust in that providence emanating from a gratuitous creation, a confession reflected later in Muslim insistence on *tawhid*: "faith in divine unity," which we have seen al-Ghazali parse effectively as trust (*tawakkul*). So both Christian and Muslim traditions extolling trust in God find their roots in the biblical "fear and love" elaborated by Moses ben Maimon, so can be considered elaboration of these prior ancestral traditions, on this subject so intimately linked.

Notes

1 Jean-Pierre de Caussade, *The Sacrament of the Present Moment* (trans. Kitty Muggeridge; San Francisco: Harper & Row, 1982); *Al-Ghazali on Faith in Divine Unity and Trust in Divine Providence* (trans. of Bk 35 of *Ihya' Ulum ad-Din* by David Burrell; Louisville, KY: Fons Vitae, 2000).

2 This section has been adapted from the Introduction to my translation, *Al-Ghazali on Faith in Divine Unity and Trust in Divine Providence*, Bk 35 of *Ihya' Ulum ad-Din* (Louisville, KY: Fons Vitae, 2000).

3 It is doubtless modish to translate "*tahafut*" as "deconstruction," but then "destruction" is not quite right either; others have suggested "stumbling." The best English translation of this work of Ghazali is by Michael Marmura, *Tahafut al-Falasifa* (Provo, UT: Brigham Young University, 2000). There is no current English (or Western language) translation of the *Magasid*, though one is proposed for the SUNY-Binghamton series under the general editorship of Parviz Morewedge. There are two Arabic versions, neither critical, one published by Muhl. ad-Din Sabri al-Kurdi, Cairo, 1331 A.H.; the other edited by Sulayman Dunya for Dar al-Ma'arif, Cairo, 1961.

4 G.-H. Bousquet, *Analyse et Index* (Paris: Max Besson, 1955).

5 See David Burrell and Nazih Daher (trans.), *Al-Ghazali: The Ninety-Nine Beautiful Names of God* (Cambridge: Islamic Texts Society, 1992).

6 ST 1.1.4: "Sacred doctrine takes over both [speculative and practical] functions, in this being like the single knowledge whereby God knows himself and the things he makes" (cf. ST 1.14.5).

7 For a sketch of that model, see my *Knowing the Unknowable God* (Notre Dame, IN: University of Notre Dame Press, 1986).

8 On the apparent connections with Ibn Sina here, see Richard M. Frank, *Creation and the Cosmic System: Ghazali and Avicenna* (Heidelberg: Carl Winter, 1992).

9 This progression is reminiscent of his autobiographical sketch, the *Munqidh min al-dalal* (English translation by R.J. McCarthy, *Freedom and Fulfillment* (Boston: Twayne, 1980; Louisville, KY: Fons Vitae, 2000)).

10 This term is not Qur'anic nor is it a name of God; cf. L.P. Fitzgerald, *Creation in al-Tafsir al-Kabir of Fakhr ad-Din al-Razi* (PhD dissertation, Australian National University, 1992), p. 34.

11 William Chittick proposes that we render *qadar* as "the measuring out," and with respect to human understanding, the "mystery of the

measuring out" – see *Faith and Practice in Islam* (Albany, NY: State University of New York Press, 1992), pp. 21, 189, 213.

12 *Al-'Adl* (Just) is a name of God (cf. *Al-Ghazali: The Ninety-Nine Beautiful Names*, pp. 92–96), and the following expression "omnipotent" is derived from the name *al-Qddir* (*Al-Ghazali: The Ninety-Nine Beautiful Names*, pp. 131–132).

13 This is Ghazali's celebrated claim regarding the universe – that it is "the best possible," a claim whose reception has been examined in detail by Eric Ormsby, *Theodicy in Islamic Thought* (Princeton, NJ: Princeton University Press, 1984), and revisited in his contribution "Creation in Time in Islamic Thought with Special Reference to al-Ghazali," in David Burrell and Bernard McGinn (eds), *God and Creation* (Notre Dame, IN: University of Notre Dame Press, 1990): See also Frank, *Creation and the Cosmic System*, pp. 60–61.

14 Ormsby, "Creation in Time," p. 256, quoting from his own *Theodicy in Islamic Thought*, pp. 32–91. Also see Ormsby, "Creation in Time," p. 257.

15 Such stories are legion; see Qushayri, *Risdla 166*, 13–14; Ansari, *Sharh ar-Risdla al-Qushayriya* 4, 173.

16 See my "Why Not Pursue the Metaphor of Artisan and View God's Knowledge as Practical?" in Lenn E. Goodman (ed.), *Neoplatonism and Jewish Thought* (Albany: State University of New York Press, 1992) pp. 207–216.

17 Ormsby, "Creation in Time," p. 256.

18 David Burrell and Elena Malits, CSC, *Original Peace: Restoring God's Creations* (New York: Paulist Press, 1997).

19 *The Kingly Crown (Keter Malkhut)* (trans. Bernard Lewis, with Introduction and commentary by Andrew Gluck; Notre Dame, IN: University of Notre Dame Press, 2003).

20 *Guide of the Perplexed*, Bk 3, ch. 42.

5

The Point of it All: "Return," Judgment, and "Second Coming" – Creation to Consummation

If creation is to have a point and not be in vain, it must strain towards some kind of consummation. For what point would an emanation from the One have without inspiring a return to that same One? And while that "return," like the original creation, will embrace all-that-is, we should also note, once again, how the "return" of intentional creatures will assume a form distinct from that of all other creatures. The Qur'an nicely articulates the reason for this: intentional creatures are "vicegerents" of creation, deputed not only to be stewards but to have a role directing all of creation to its proper end. It is fair to say that this pattern of emanation/ return (*exitus/redditus*), redolent of Plotinus, can be found in each of these three traditions. It is the master-plan of Aquinas's *Summa Theologiae* as well as the key to Islamic philosophical theology from al-Farabi and Avicenna (Ibn Sina) to Mulla Sadra (Sadr al-Din al-Shirazi) in seventeenth-century Iran. Jewish thinkers, Moses Maimonides and Ibn Gabirol, have articulated these issues in prose and verse. We shall see how modalities of "redemption"

Towards a Jewish-Christian-Muslim Theology, First Edition. David B. Burrell.
© 2011 John Wiley & Sons Ltd. Published 2011 by John Wiley & Sons Ltd.

invariably relate to original creation. Christian eschatology focuses mainly on Jesus' "second coming," with a final judgment ushering in the eschaton, while Jewish reflection tends to coincide with the "Messianic era" rather than focus so clearly on a "last judgment," and Islam elaborates a scenario of resurrection linked to the final judgment determining all destinies. Yet they each share a keen sense that this remains "undiscovered country," as Peter Hawkins entitles his explorations via Dante's *Commedia*.[1]

So whatever is said about the end-of-it-all will at best take the form of commentary on scriptural depictions which are manifestly prophetic in character, posed in language which may inflame or explode, but is clearly not intended to be straightforward description, none of which can be made available. So it appears that we must take our bearings on this undiscovered country from what we are told of the setting and import of creation. But that too is quite beyond our reach, lacking any witnesses. So these two framing "events" will come to illuminate each other, since nothing we know can illuminate either of them independently. All this poses immense epistemological issues, of course, so there is little wonder that hermeneutics takes over. It can easily assume an esoteric mode, as Mulla Sadra exhibits in moving from sober philosophical argument to parsing texts in an eschatological fashion, in his *Divine Manifestations of the Secrets of the Perfecting Sciences*.[2] Short of that exuberance, each tradition will focus on the *way*, the *path*, to show how the end can be present now, as a transcendent destination illuminating our way by giving this path a point. Yet precisely because the destination can be "known" only by faith, it remains a journey in hope. And a hope rooted in the One God's freely creating the universe, so presaging a final resurrection which culminates it.

A fascinating parallel between the New Testament and Qur'an can be found in comparing Peter's allusion to the illuminating power of scripture in the New Testament with the celebrated "light verse" of the Qur'an:

> You will do well to pay attention to it, because it is like a lamp shining in a dark place until the day dawns and the light of the morning star rises in your hearts (1 Pet. 1:18).

God is the light of the heavens and the earth. Here is how we may conceive of His light – a lamp is set in a niche where, encased in glass which glistens with the very brilliance of a star, it is kindled from the oil of the olive, a blessed tree, which is confined neither to the east nor to the west. Its oil is almost luminous without the touch of fire. Light upon light, God guides to his light whom He wills and God, who knows all things, gives to mankind the thoughts by which to ponder His ways (24:35–38).

These texts have inspired faithful in each tradition to discover ways to let their scriptures enter into their minds and hearts, so as to transform them into people who walk God-given ways to proximity with God.

We can identify the following eschatological motifs, echoing free creation, in Islam: the "Primordial Covenant," the promised transformation of the natural order as we know it (Sura 81), and a "second creation" in the resurrection of the body with a final judgment.[3] Adopting a more philosophical idiom, the Shi'ite philosophical theologian Mulla Sadra cites Ibn 'Arabi to insist that every being is oriented in its basic activity of existing/living towards its creator, as "they abide in the primordial disposition concerning the unity of God [*tawhîd*]. ... This is worship by [one's] essence: ... all the natural movements and transferences in the essences of the natures of souls are towards God, by God, and in the way of God. Man by his innate disposition travels towards Him."[4] So human beings are the *vicegerents* of creation by rendering articulate what all things "say" by their very activity. Yet we would never be able to hear what things "say" unless we let God's word in the Qur'an unveil the inner orientation to their creator of realities surrounding us:

Now the existence of each thing is delightful in itself, and were [each thing] to attain to the existence which causes it by bringing it into being, it would be [assimilated to] that by which it has its existence, so its delight would be perfect in appropriating [all that]. To the extent that existences differ ... the felicity [associated with intellectual ability] will be more intense, for their pleasure and passionate love is more perfect. So our souls, with their inherent goals and

89

powers ... return to their true identity when the One originating them will bestow on them a delight and felicity impossible to describe or to compare with sensible pleasure. ... God takes their souls and natures by forelock, and He is the one who turns them towards Him and attracts them towards Him. The one who realizes this will have the certainty of the necessity of the Return of all, and will have no doubt about that. That is the requisite of the wisdom and the fulfilment of the [divine] promise and threat, the necessity of reward and recompense (p. 526).

By adroit allusions to Qur'anic language, Mulla Sadra uses philosophical tools to show how Qur'anic language can offer a primary source of wisdom. Moreover, he does so by reinforcing the fundamental Qur'anic rhythm of *emanation* and *return* (*exitus/redditus*), rather than by appealing to esoteric modes of interpretation.

In fact, Mulla Sadra privileges philosophical discourse precisely "because the Sufi habit is to be confined to only the taste [i.e., mystical experience – *dhawq*] and heart-knowledge in what they judge, but we do not rely on anything for which there is no definite demonstration" (p. 560). So his careful description of a resurrected state, so reminiscent of Dante's *Commedia*, will try to codify images gleaned from the Qur'an:

The resurrection of creatures will be of different kinds, depending on the acts, habitudes and opinions: ... *that Day we shall gather the God-fearing towards the Beneficent as a group* (19:85) [while] *the enemies of God will be raised to Hell* (41:1). ... In brief, each one according to his ultimate effort, his act, what he loves and craves, even if he loves a stone, will be resurrected with it (p. 553). [For] in the interior of every man and deeply rooted inside him is [a living being] subsisting in act, [which] does not die at the death of the body. It will be raised on the Day of Resurrection in the form corresponding to its inner content. It is this who will be rewarded and punished; ... its life is essential like the life of the soul ... intermediate between the intellective and sensory animal. It will be raised on the Day of Resurrection in the form of dispositions and habitudes, which the soul acquires by its practical hand (p. 554).

At this point he endorses the bold statement of Shaykh Muhy al-Din al-'Arabi (Ibn 'Arabi):

> the quintessence of divine knowledge is to know that you at this very moment are like that, resurrecting at every breath in the form of the state in which you are (p. 560).

So Mulla Sadra's eschatology, like that of Ibn 'Arabi, is thoroughly "realized eschatology." In fact, the "state" of resurrected being is inherently dynamic, intensifying the multiple dyings and risings "of those traveling towards God."

> It is said they are like the number of breaths. This is sound according to us from the demonstration which we gave that there is nothing from the natural substances at rest in the world, especially the human substance which is moving in its essence towards the next world, the towards the Divine Presence (p. 562).

Echoing Ibn 'Arabi, Mulla Sadra summarizes how

> all the natural movements and transferences in the essences of the natures and souls are towards God, by God, and in the way of God. Man by his innate disposition travels towards him. But in regard to his choice and caprice, if he is from the felicitous people he will increase in his nearness [to God] some proximity [to Him], and in his innate wayfaring some effort, assiduity and swiftness.

Contrasting "felicitous people" with those, "like beasts and brutes, who do not comprehend anything except animal goals" (p. 670), we can come to see why types so disparate would attain such disparate ends, and how acquired dispositions presage the quality of their goals. No need for any forensic judgment; what will be results from what has been the case, though the eschaton will render the ineluctable process manifest.

Judaism, for its part, strains towards resurrection, variously depicted as culminating the "original peace" of creation.[5] As in Islam, creation *ex nihilo* presages resurrection, as one offers testimony for the other, so obviating the need to "prove" either one. As we have seen already, however, when Jon Levenson offers a biblical picture of creation as the counterpoint of resurrection, he will carefully sidestep *ex nihilo*:

> The possibility of resurrection – the raising of the body by God – is thus … rooted in the power of God at creation. If God could raise Adam out of dust, then he can surely raise a dead body at the general resurrection. The victory of God over death at the end … mirrors the primordial victory of the God of life at the beginning and reminds us that we owe our lives, before death and after, to the God who created all. We do not live, and we will not live again, by nature alone (p. 41).

Nevertheless, Hebrew Scriptures are seldom keen on individual resurrection ("except in rare and noteworthy circumstances"), preferring to focus on the legacy rooted in progeny and in lasting good deeds. The theology imbedded in the Hebrew Scriptures is one "in which the fact of death and the promise of life, each of them of capital importance, stand in a relationship of tension" (p. 169), much like the creator facing chaos.

Yet Levenson uses Dan. 12:1–3 to remind us that "the last word lies not with death … but with life":

> At that time the great prince, Michael, who stands beside the sons of your people, will appear. It will be a time of trouble, the like of which has never been since the nation came into being. At that time, your people will be rescued, all who are found inscribed in the book. Many of those that sleep in the dust of the earth will awake, some to eternal life, others to reproaches, to everlasting abhorrence. And the wise will be radiant like the bright expanse of sky, and those who lead the many to righteousness will be like the stars forever and ever.

So "given the reality and potency ascribed to death throughout the Hebrew Bible, what overcomes is nothing short of the most astonishing miracle, the Divine Warrior's eschatological victory" (p. 200), recapitulating creation prevailing over chaos. Levenson goes on to show how Reformed Jewry altered their prayer books to turn this forthright resolution in favor of life into a metaphor, so reinstating the more sober reading of the Hebrew Scriptures in favor of an individual legacy rooted in progeny and lasting good deeds. As a result, Jewish tradition has attenuated the stark Muslim focus on judgment and resurrection, to say nothing of Christian emphasis on individual postmortem destiny, thereby rendering resurrection of any sort "the least known teaching in Judaism" (pp. 201–220). Maimonides even conspired "to make resurrection superfluous," as his neo-Platonic propensities led him to a strange teaching whereby "those resurrected … will undergo a second death, from which they will never arise in bodily form" (p. 214). Yet Levenson notes how, in "early Christian writings … the identity of the God of creation with the God of resurrection is underscored virtually everywhere" (p. 229), recapitulating a constant theme of the Hebrew Scriptures and dramatizing it in the ritual of baptism (pp. 235–245).

Christianity exhibits in various ways how fitting it is that what has come forth bear fruit in returning to its source. From Clement of Rome at the end of the first century, we hear quite simply: "To God we owe everything, and therefore on every count we are under the obligation to return thanks to him."[6] Or from Columban, an Irish monk missioned to Europe in the sixth century:

[the] great dignity that God bestowed upon us [in creation is] the image of his eternity and the likeness of his character. A grand distinction for us is the likeness of God, if it be preserved. If we employ the virtues planted in our soul to a proper end, we will be like to God. So whatever virtues God sowed in us in our original state, he taught us in the commandments to restore the same to him.[7]

Columban then invokes scriptural warrant to identify specific things we have received, so are enjoined to return by developing in ourselves: love, holiness, righteousness, and truth, "since he is righteous and true." Yet the fact that these are implanted in us from creation reminds us that their development stems not from us but from that originating creative impulse – all is grace.

So there is a clear Abrahamic consensus that free creation elicits a reciprocal return. But what assures that will happen? And how might it happen? In Torah and the Qur'an Jews and Muslims are each given a "straight path" to follow. But the ways of the world remain seductive and compelling for us humans, whose activities are often fueled by resentment. Witness the obscene ways the memories of the victims of Nazi extermination have been distorted to justify actions which qualify for universal condemnation on the part of a new "Jewish state." For even when such actions are condemned, "the Holocaust" provides the convenient cover of a victim role. Or with Islam, the humiliation which came and continues to come from a Zionism which solicits uncritical support for illegal state actions offers a twisted motivation to carry out indiscriminate killings of innocent people. At this point Christians will invoke the crucified Jesus, as a way of understanding the persistence of evil in the world, as well as motivating believers to act according to the Abrahamic consensus. Yet the fact that the cross itself was purportedly central to a vision in which Constantine was assured "in this sign you shall conquer" enemies of the empire, only shows how any religious symbol can be refurbished to serve power. (In the Epilog I shall try to assess these painful betrayals of and by each tradition in a final and inescapably painful retrospective.)

Yet if we ask why Jesus' death and resurrection are so central to Christian faith, we may well be offered a theory (attributed to Anselm) whereby God ("the Father") requires ultimate "satisfaction" for the sins of humankind. But this answer effectively subverts the "crucified" in yet another way: by reducing the polyvalent symbol of the cross to a theory, and one which presumes to speculate about the motives and *modus operandi* of a God whose ways are acknowledged to be inscrutable. Yet other ways of illuminating this notorious stumbling block have been offered, so let us consider one of them to show how this signal difference may also lead to mutual understanding. In his landmark work, *The Crucified Jesus Is No Stranger*, Sebastian Moore employs human psychology to integrate some key scriptural texts: "if I am lifted up…"; "they looked upon him whom they had pierced"; to underscore the part reserved to all

present – young and old – in the dramatic reading of the gospel for
Good Friday: "Crucify him!" From Holy Week in Jerusalem I treas-
ure the Anglican canon who responded to the disputed question:
"who killed Jesus, the Romans or the Jews?" with "I should have
thought that any Christian who tried to attribute Jesus' death on
someone else has missed the point of the gospel!" So the crucified
Jesus is hardly a stranger to us since we all participated in his
demise. Why and how? Because Jesus' very presence upsets our
well-laid plans to avoid any serious reckoning of our actions, as the
gospels make abundantly clear. So we will collude – in fantasy or
in fact – with eliminating that disturbing presence by whatever
means we can find. Yet should we dare turn about to face the crucified sinless one, recognizing that we would have done it had we
been able, we will be brought to a self-knowledge that is so rare that
we wonder whether there could be any other way of attaining it.

For God's love has no way to our heart except through repentance, yet given how endemic self-deception is to us, some dramatic
action was required. An analog may be found in Gandhi's nonviolent campaign for Indian independence from the British imperial
power. Repression of indigenous people had become a fact of colonial life in a thousand institutional ways, but Gandhi created a
dramatic encounter between unarmed people protesting that sub-
jugation that revealed colonialism's inhuman face so starkly that
some of those who had been unwitting accessories to such policies
could no longer hide that fact from themselves. The use of violence
on the part of the Indian people, however, would have provided an
excuse for colonials continuing their denial. This way of interpreting the "passion narrative" presumes the hand of God as well, but
as a master strategist who knows and loves us as only our creator
can, rather than a despot intent on "satisfaction." As with the bulk
of India's British masters, the ruse may fail to elicit repentance, but
no form of coercion could get us onto "the straight path" either. Yet
this ruse respects our freedom while addressing our endemic self-
deception as well. We are reminded of Syriac allusions to the crucifixion as a crafty way of deceiving the devil to snatch victory from
the powers of evil and death, yet those powers are now firmly

ensconced in us, explaining how affronting the presence of this sinless one must be in the midst of a world we have tailored to our satisfaction.

On readings like this, "the crucifixion"' and "the crucified one" become a genial way for a merciful God to try to elicit from free creatures that modicum of honesty required to return the gift of their existence and of creation itself to the One from whom they receive it. If that is what each of these traditions seeks, Jesus' way offers one answer to the query: how might free creatures be brought to respond to the gift of creation by returning all to the One from whom we have received all? Repentance (*teshuva*) is the key to activating a loving God to grant the forgiveness which can empower us to undertake that return. Anyone who has participated in Jewish high holydays will be overwhelmed by ceaseless Yom Kippur imprecations for God's forgiveness, yet the repetition drives home a crucial point: as inattentive as we have been all year, how can we dare to expect divine forgiveness? So we implore once more. Yet Christians believe that Jesus, "the crucified one," pleads with the God of Israel, whom he addresses as "Father," for "all of God's people" (Jn 12:24). So there is no need to keep imploring God, once those people have tasted Jesus' vulnerability to the point of confessing their need for the forgiveness which the Father surely grants them. So "the crucifixion" has two faces; one directed to human beings to capture their attention, with the other towards God (as Jesus' father) to respond favorably to the contrition elicited. Note how this analysis of the signal event renders both irrelevant and distracting a purported divine demand for a bloody sacrifice to offer "satisfaction" (to this God?) for the sin of mankind. Bloody sacrifice it is, of course, yet designed to bring a recalcitrant humanity to the point of recognizing – individually and corporately – our complicity in the reign of sin over the world. Only then will we be in a position to begin to return all to the One from whom we have received all.

How can Judaism or Islam address our principal query to the clear Abrahamic consensus that free creation elicits a reciprocal return: what assures that will happen? And how might it happen? In each tradition, what responds to that question seems to be the conviction that the community will never lack faithful whose lives exemplify that "return," so will be able to attract backsliders ("hypocrites") to reform their wayward lives. Moses or Muhammad were offered as exemplary individuals in a foundational sense, to be sure, but their example will have to be repeated for each generation tempted to forsake the "straight path." God's gracious care for a particular people, chosen by genealogy or through a response in faith, will be manifested in the continual presence of exemplary models for executing the return. These are the "just ones" among Jews, those "in proximity to God" among Muslims, and those acclaimed as "saints" among Christians, as the pattern of Jesus' life, death, and resurrection comes to be replicated in those living among us in each generation. Every encounter with these exemplars of a tradition counts as a "special grace" of the God who creates and sustains us, reminding us how community links us intentionally with the creator.

How does "proximity with God" work? Each of the Abrahamic traditions has had to struggle with the relation between a creator's freedom and that of creatures, as we have seen. Let us look at some of the most radical statements of this intimate relationship, to see how they might illuminate one another.

Hope beyond our Capacity to Hope: John of the Cross and Edith Stein[8]

We have all been gifted with teachers and guides, companions and friends, present to us whether currently living or not, who shape our lives by giving us the courage to live and to love. The letters of Edith Stein, as daughter, student, companion, teacher, and then as Teresa Benedicta of the Cross, testify to a person replete with friends, nourished by relationships which she herself cultivated.[9] Responding to the initial invitation of another Teresa to collaborate in the reform of Carmel, John of the Cross devoted the bulk of his life as a religious to that work, carrying out assigned duties in the order despite acute and recriminatory opposition, yet never allowed any of it to displace his vocation as a spiritual guide. Indeed, his two most lyrical works, *The Spiritual Canticle* and *The Living Flame of Love*, were composed at the behest of friends who had come to accompany him in the spirit: Ana de Jesús and Doña Ana de Peñalosa, respectively.[10]

The plot thickens as Edith Stein, also called forth on the journey which led her to become Sister Teresa Benedicta by her encounter with Teresa de Avila, devotes what were to be the final months of her life attempting "to understand John of the Cross in his life and works, considering him from a point of view that enables us to envisage this unity." Occasioned by the then impending fourth centenary of John, this philosopher would seize that opportunity to "penetrate to the unity" of John's life and works, incorporating "an interpretation, offering what she believes a lifetime of effort to have taught her about the lows of intellectual and spiritual being and life." So she will not hesitate to expound "her theories on sprit, faith and contemplation," specifying that "what [she says] on ego, freedom and person is not derived from the writings of our holy Father John ... for only modern philosophy has set itself the task of working out a philosophy of the person such as is suggested in the passages just mentioned."[11] This relationship of master-disciple, sustained by the family of Carmel extended over space and time, allows the apprentice to exercise her own experience coupled to philosophical developments achieved in the intervening four centuries. So the relationship between these two – a poet with an exquisite grasp of matters in philosophical theology, and a vigorous philosopher brought through her interior life to a refined sensibility for the poetics of love – can epitomize our thesis about the fruitfulness of lives lived in so rich a community of prayer and inquiry.

To help us appreciate the homage of this philosophical spirit to her poetic guide and predecessor in Carmel, let us consider a work completed a few years before, *Finite and Eternal Being: Attempting an Ascent to the Meaning of Being*, which followed her self-imposed task of appropriating the thought of Thomas Aquinas by translating his *Disputed Questions on Truth*. The later synthetic work on the metaphysics of Aquinas owes an express gratitude to Erich

Przywara's *Analogia Entis*, a work which presaged the fruitful efforts of Louis Geiger and Cornelius Fabro to call attention to the centrality of *participation* in the metaphysics of Thomas Aquinas.[12] What is remarkable about Edith Stein's inquiry is her ability to penetrate to the heart of Aquinas's subtle and elusive discourse on *being*, and do so without the benefit of the studies cited; indeed without much reliance on secondary literature at all. Yet her own confessed formation in the "school of Edmund Husserl ... and phenomenological method" may have offered her a prescient optic for the potencies of Aquinas language in trying to bring to expression this axial notion of metaphysics which in fact resists any proper conceptual formation.[13]

But let us first try to evoke the rich person of this scholar who found herself so drawn by truth as it was unveiled to her, as well as drawn to those with whom she shared this adventure: friends and students (who quickly became friends) alike. Gifted with a thoroughly intellectual temperament, her advice to a colleague, Fritz Kaufmann, reveals as well just how centered she already was at 28 (in 1919):

> I am worried at seeing how, for months, you have avoided doing purely philosophical work, and am gradually beginning to wonder whether your "profession" should not lie in a different direction. Please do not take this as a vote of "no confidence" or as doubting your ability. I only mean that one should not use force to make the center of one's life anything that fails to give one the right kind of satisfaction.[14]

Equally drawn as she was to scholarship and to guiding others to cognate goals, she could be utterly forthright in critique of another's work, as evidenced in her response to Maria Bruck's dissertation comparing two German philosophers:

> I am convinced that if you have an opportunity to work for a few years longer at systematic philosophy, you will yourself experience the need to go beyond [this work]; not merely take an independent position on the problems you have touched but, above all, to tackle

the interpretation from the basis of clearly established final principles. Without that, no actual comparison of what is meant as systematic philosophy is possible. From the start I missed a sharp delineation of what Brentano and Husserl understood as the *real* and as *essence*, and several other matters.[15]

To be sure, this communication begins gently: "Undoubtedly this work demanded a great deal of effort from you. It is very neat and conscientious and will surely be of lasting use for anyone who will study the relationship of Husserl to Brentano"; but its author cannot have failed to discern, in her friend Edith's words, that she had rather missed the point – philosophically.

In a more personal vein, to a former student who was herself discerning a vocation to religious life, Edith writes:

> God leads each of us on an individual way; one reaches the goal more easily and more quickly than another. We can do very little ourselves, compared to what is done to us. But that little bit we must do. Primarily, this consists before all else of persevering in prayer to find the right way, and of following without resistance the attraction of grace when we feel it. Whoever acts in this way and perseveres patiently will not be able to say that his efforts were in vain. But one may not set a deadline for the Lord. ... Among the books you got as a child, do you have Andersen's Fairy Tales? If so, read the story of the ugly duckling. I believe in your swan-destiny. (Section 102)

And to another former student, now teaching in school, also discerning religious life, she writes:

> To contend for souls and love them in the Lord is the Christian's duty and, actually, a special goal of the Dominican Order. But if that is your goal and if the thought of marriage is farthest from your mind, then it will be good if you soon begin to wear appropriate dress. That will make it clear to people who it is they are dealing with. Otherwise there will be the danger of your misleading others, of your behavior being misinterpreted. (I would be surprised if, without your being aware of it, that has not already happened at times.), and your achieving exactly the opposite of what you desire. (Section 103)

It should be clear how those who associated with this woman could be assured of hearing the truth as she saw it, yet at the same time many seemed ineluctably drawn to her, as she reminds her colleague Fritz (in 1931):

> The circle of persons whom I consider as connected with me has increased to much in the course of the years that it is entirely impossible to keep in touch by the usual means. But I have other ways and means of keeping the bonds alive. (Section 93a)

Edith had been thwarted early on from pursuing her second doctorate (*Habilitationschrift*) for the simple reason that she was a woman, and her remarks (again to Fritz Kaufmann) on the academic politics surrounding the matter were unyielding (Section 31). Yet within two weeks, she finds herself consoling him:

> It was terribly dear of you to be so zealous on my behalf, but I must tell you that things have gone very well for me in the past weeks and that I am no longer the least bit furious or sad. Instead I find the whole matter very funny. After all, I do not consider life on the whole to carry so much weight that it would matter a great deal what position I occupy. And I would like you to make that attitude your own (Section 32).

She realized perfectly well that she would never be admitted to university teaching without the second doctorate, yet service was already more important than a career, so she soon immersed herself in secondary teaching at a Dominican Sisters' school in Speyer (Bavaria) soon after her baptism on January 1, 1922 (at 31) – a position she held for nine years until she resigned to complete her translation of Aquinas. All during this time she immersed herself in lectures on the place of women, especially in Catholic circles, remarking in 1931: "During my years in the *Gymnasium* and as a young student [at the university] I was a radical feminist. Then I lost interest in the whole question. Now, because I am obliged to do so, I seek purely objective solutions" (Section 100). Fully engaged in teaching young women, she made their concerns her own, yet in a quite disinterested way. This vocational commitment was, if anything, intensified in her next post at the *Deutsches Institut für Wissenschaftliche Pädagogik* (German Institute for Scientific Pedagogy), from where she continued to lecture on women's issues until 1933 when the National Socialists insisted that Jews be deprived of teaching posts. Writing again to Fritz Kaufmann, she is able to say that

> the *umsturz* was for me a sign from heaven that I might now go the way that I had long considered as mine. After a final visit with my relatives in Breslau and a difficult farewell from my dear mother, I entered the monastery of the Carmelite nuns here last Saturday and thus became a daughter of St. Teresa, who earlier inspired me to conversion. (Section 158a)

In that life she would be able to pursue her interior vocation intellectually as well, and be prepared for the ultimate test, to come in less than a decade.

From what we have seen of Edith Stein, we would be hard-pressed to read her move to Carmel as "leaving the world," but rather as intensifying her presence to a world gone mad. Indeed, her letters from Breslau to her friends, on the cusp of entering Carmel, invite them all to visit her there, while reflections in an earlier (1928) letter to a Dominican sister friend help us to read the move more accurately:

> Immediately before, and for a good while after my conversion, I was of the opinion that to lead a religious life meant one had to give up all that was secular and to live totally immersed in thoughts of the Divine. But gradually I realized that something else is asked of us in this world and that, even in the contemplative life, one may not sever the connection with the world. I even believe that the deeper one is drawn into God, the more one must "go out of oneself": that is, one must go to the world in order to carry the divine life into it. The only essential is that one finds, first of all, a quiet corner in which one can communicate with God as though there were nothing else, and that must be done daily. ... Furthermore, [it is essential] that one accept

one's particular mission there, preferably for each day, and not make one's own choice. Finally, one is to consider oneself totally as an instrument, especially with regard to the abilities one uses to perform one's special tasks, in our case, e.g., intellectual ones. We are to see them as something used, not by us, but by God in us. ... My life begins anew each morning, and ends every evening; I have neither plans nor prospects beyond it. (Section 45)

As we shall see, it would be difficult to find a better formula for describing a life patterned on the transformation outlined by John of the Cross; Edith seemed to have been prepared to move quite naturally into Sister Teresa Benedicta of the Cross.

While she did not complete her constructive monograph on the unity of John's life and work until her final days, we can easily discern her pull to Carmel, first in her attraction to Teresa of Avila, and then in her inner affinity for the purity of John of the Cross's presentation of the inner dynamics of a life of faith. John is disarmingly forthright in identifying the goal of that journey: "the union and transformation of the [person] in God" (*Ascent of Mount Carmel* 2.5.3); as well as the means: "faith alone, which is the only proximate and proportionate means to union with God" (2.9.1). He is at pains to distinguish this intentional union from the "union between God and creatures [which] always exists [by which] God sustains every soul and dwells in it substantially. ... By it He conserves their being so that if the union would end they would immediately be annihilated and cease to exist" (2.5.3). So John will presume the unique metaphysical relation of all creatures to their source which Meister Eckhart elaborated from Aquinas's "distinction," and does not hesitate it to call it a *union* – indeed, an "essential or substantial union." This grounding fact attends all creatures, hence it is *natural* and found in everything (though displayed differently in animate from inanimate, and in animate, differs from animals to humans, though among humans it can still be found in "the greatest sinner in the world"), while the intentional union is *supernatural* and can only be found "where there is a likeness of love [such that] God's will and the [person's] are in conformity" (2.5.3).

We shall see that what eliminates any prospect of "heteronomy" between those two wills is precisely this "non-reciprocal relation of dependence" which attends all creatures, but let us attend first to the internal connection between *faith* and *union* which John confidently asserts. What makes this sound so startling is our propensity to confine such talk to "mystics," while reducing faith to belief: holding certain propositions to be true. This is a long and complex debate in Christian theology, which often cuts oddly across confessional lines, so the best we can do here is to remind ourselves that John of the Cross could well have been responding from the Iberian Peninsula to sixteenth-century winds from northern Europe. He does so by elaborating some key assertions of Aquinas to cut through the debates which polarized intellect and will in the act of faith.

First, Aquinas: "Faith is a sort of knowledge [*cognitio quaedam*] in that it makes the mind assent to something. The assent is not due to what is seen by the believer but to what is seen by him who is believed" (*Summa Theologiae* (ST) 1.12.13.3). The one who is believed is, of course, the Word of God incarnate, Jesus, as mediated through the Scriptures, so this peculiar "sort of knowledge" is rooted in an interpersonal relation of the believer with Jesus. It is that relation, at the root of faith, which John of the Cross sets out to explore, quite aware that what results from it will "fall short of the mode of knowing [*cognitio*] which is properly called 'knowledge' [*scientia*], for such knowledge causes the mind to assent through what is seen and through an understanding of first principles" (ST 1.12.13.3). More positively, Aquinas will characterize faith as "an act of mental assent commanded by the will, [so] to believe perfectly our mind must tend unfailingly towards the perfection of truth, in unfailing service of that ultimate goal for the sake of which our will is commanding our mind's assent" (ST 2–2.4.5). Unlike ordinary belief, then, faith must be an act of the whole person, involving a personal and critical quest for a truth which outreaches our proper expression. John will focus critically on our concepts: "nothing which could possibly be imagined or comprehended in this life can be a proximate means of union with God" (*Ascent of Mount Carmel* 2.8.4), since "nothing created or imagined can serve the intellect as a proper means for union with God; [rather], all that can be grasped by the intellect would serve as an obstacle rather than a means, if a person were to become attached to it" (2.8.1).

So following Aquinas's lead, we must be able to let our conceptualities "lead us on by the hand" (*manuductio*), as John does, to a goal which transcends them.[16] That goal, we recall, is "union and transformation of the [person] in God," already intimated in the sort of *faith* which Thomas and John envisage. As Augustine had already worked it out, Christian faith differs from ordinary belief in being a response to an utterly gratuitous invitation, which could never be initiated by persons themselves. So this treatment of faith and union anticipates the critiques of both Freud and Marx, while leaving room for both. For if Freud would belittle religious faith as projections, Aquinas does not hesitate to say that "faith that does not rely on divine truth can fail and believe falsehood" (ST 2–2.4.5). Yet if we regard John of the Cross as developing Aquinas's lapidary exposition of faith, authentic faith will ever involve a journey of responding rather than initiating, with distracting projections facing a searing critique. And with regard to Marx, it is John's forthright insistence on *union* which responds to Marx's characterization of Christian faith as alienating human beings from their authentic life and work by offering a distracting "heavenly reward," for the union of which John speaks begins now. Yet Marx's account may well address a Christian ethos quite innocent of the tradition John articulates: an internal connection between faith and union. So Marx's critique can well inspire the kind of internal critique which John's account of faith demands. Indeed, the demands of that journey of faith which John outlines are utterly rigorous: "we shall explain how in order to journey to God the intellect must be perfected in the darkness of faith, the memory in the emptiness of hope, and the will in the nakedness and absence of every affection [unrelated to the goal of union]" (2.6.1).

A poetic characterization of that intentional union is offered in his *Living Flame of Love*, where we can cite the initial stanza of the poem together with statements from his own commentary.

> O living flame of love
> That tenderly wounds my soul
> In its deepest center! Since
> Now You are not oppressive,
> Now Consummate! If it be your will:
> Tear through the veil of this sweet encounter!

The commentary begins:

> The soul now feels that it all inflamed in the divine union ... and that in the most intimate part of its substance it is flooded with no less than rivers of glory, abounding in delights, and that from its bosom flow rivers of living waters [Jn 7:38], which the Son of God declared will rise up in such souls. Accordingly it seems, because it is so vigorously transformed in God, so sublimely possessed by Him, and arrayed with such rich gifts and virtues, that it is singularly close to beatitude – so close that only a thin veil separates it" (1.1).

> This flame of love is the Spirit of the Bridegroom, which is the Holy Spirit. ... Such is the activity of the Holy Spirit in the soul transformed in love: the interior acts He produces shoot up flames for they are acts of inflamed love, in which the will of the soul united with that flame, made one with it, loves most sublimely. ... Thus in this state the soul cannot make acts because the Holy Spirit makes them all and moves it towards them. As a result all the acts of the soul are divine, since the movement toward these acts and their execution stems from God. Hence it seems to a person that every time this flame shoots up, making him love with delight and divine quality, it is giving him eternal life, since it raises him up to the activity of God in God. (1.3–4)

There is no hint of "heteronomy" here, I would suggest, because John presumes that unique metaphysical relation of person ("soul") to its source which Meister Eckhart develops from Aquinas.

Sister Teresa Benedicta had become attuned to that unique relation of creatures to their creator in her study of Aquinas on eternal and temporal being, which led her into the presence of the great mystery of creation: that God has called forth each being into its differentiated being; a manifold of beings in which what is one in God is there separate. ... [Yet] the subsistence of creatures is no longer that of a portrait over against the one portrayed, or of a work over against the artist doing it. Earlier [thinkers] had likened the relation to that of a mirror to the object in the mirror, or of refracted light to its pure source, yet these remain but imperfect images for what is quite incomparable.[17]

She then goes on to compare the creator/creature relation to the relations among the divine "persons":

The entire divine essence is common to all three persons. So what remains is simply the differences of the persons as such: a perfect unity of *we*, which no community of finite persons could ever realize, yet in this unity the difference of *I* from *you* remains, without which no *we* is possible. ... Indeed, the *we* as the unity of *I* and *you* – "I and the Father are one" (Jn 10:30) – is a higher unity than the *I*. For in its most perfect sense, it is the unity of love. Now love as assent to a good is possible as the self-love of an *I*, but love is more than such an assent, more than a "valuing." It is gift of oneself to the *thou*, and in its perfection – on the strength of manifold gifts of self – an existential unity [*Einssein*]. Since God is love, divine being must be an existential unity of a multiplicity of persons, while the divine name "I am" is identical in meaning with "I give myself totally to you," "I am one with a *you*," and so also identical with "we are." The love of the life interior to God can never be replaced, however, by the love between God and creatures, which can never attain love in its highest perfection – even when it be realized in the richest perfection of glory. For the highest love is differentiated eternal love: God loves creatures from eternity, whereas God can never be loved by them from eternity. (pp. 323–324)

So while the *we* of human lovers may offer an image for divine triunity, it will always fall short of that eternal unity; yet since the relation of creatures to creator also defies representation, the unity with God to which humans can be elevated by grace may be likened to that within the triune God, even though the one can never replace the other. What is incomparable can nonetheless be compared! That is the paradox into which the analogical metaphysics of Aquinas invites us, and to which the poetic genius of John of the Cross will give its most proper expression. For his poetry gives voice to the utterly unique "distinction" of creatures from creator, which we have seen John already calling a "union" in the nature of created things with their creator, and one which becomes intentionally to those who permit the interior transformation by the Holy Spirit into "images of God" become "images of Christ." In this way the circumincession of human and divine which characterizes Jesus can be bestowed upon human agents who have been turned into lovers.

So did Edith Stein, now Sister Teresa Benedicta of the Cross, trace the divine becoming so aptly described by John of the Cross in her life and works, as he had limned it in his, that her apprenticeship to him reflects ours to them both, in the circumincession of emulation which characterizes a community of revelation, as friendships sustain each of us in our search for Truth as we attempt to incorporate that Truth into the truth of our lives.

Ibn 'Arabi and Meister Eckhart

Contemporary Muslim and Christian authors, fascinated with parallels between Ibn 'Arabi and Meister Eckhart, have begun to explore their inner affinity in ways pertinent to our set task of tracing how principal protagonists of these traditions have been negotiating identical intractable theological issues in similar ways.[18] Indeed, the affinity between these two intellectual and spiritual masters can be traced to a theological appropriation of that original affinity noted in *Nostra Aetate*, the Vatican II document which opened paths of mutual illumination we have been exploring: that Jews, Christians, and Muslims each claim, from their respective faiths, that the universe is freely created by one God. This astounding assertion had initially been elaborated among medieval masters, al-Ghazali, Moses Maimonides, and Thomas Aquinas, but it fell to their successors, Ibn 'Arabi and Meister Eckhart, to mine the *sui generis* relation ensuing between creator and creatures for its philosophical and spiritual implications.[19] Yet it is telling that each of these magisterial figures has tested the limits of tolerance of their respective communities, specifically regarding the challenge of articulating the creator-creature relation. More conceptually minded philosophers of religion find their mode of apprehension and of articulation "too mystical," while respective authorities feel that each may compromise "the distinction" between creator and creatures in underscoring how unique a relation it must be. In a fascinating collusion, both philosophers and religious authorities register a concern lest "ordinary believers" be confused. Yet as we shall see, both Ibn 'Arabi and Meister Eckhart attend scrupulously to "the *distinction*" precisely to show us how creator and creatures can never be *separated*. In fact, it would be hard to find a more telling illustration of our project than the inner affinity between these two thinkers. Yet we can at best sketch here the results of these remarkable studies.

Robert Dobie's sustained thesis is that both Ibn 'Arabi and Eckhart were steeped in their respective revelational traditions, and from that vantage point engaged in a mode of philosophical theology using reason to order and clarify the revelational sources, and in turn using those sources to expand standard philosophical categories to negotiate the known perils of discourse regarding divinity. Each of these thinkers, working in disparate traditions, proceeded dialectically to allow reason and revelation to illuminate each other fruitfully. Dobie accomplishes this in four areas: revelation itself, existence, intellect, and the ideal human paradigm; in such a way as to allow each to illuminate the other, yet never eliding difference, especially where difference itself may further illuminate the comparative inquiry.

Regarding revelation, Dobie displays how "the thought of Ibn 'Arabi is inseparable from the Qur'an" (p. 25), yet "the meaning of revelation is found in the faculty of imagination, the ability to strike similitudes for what transcends reason" (p. 27). So "the imagery of the Qur'an is not a drawback for the rational seeker but an advantage, for through the 'imaginal world' … of the Qur'an and the Prophet … the inner meaning of creation manifests itself in and through a creative appropriation of that imaginal world by the believer" (p. 28). So the "seeker" in question will be one seeking an understanding which consists in conformity with the Word of God. In fact, "creation as an act of imagination is crucial to an understanding of the relation between the 'book of nature' and the 'divine book of revelation,' [so that] knowing essentially involves interpretation: we read the meaning of creation through the Names revealed to us in the Qur'an. The divine Names have causal powers, manifesting creation as God's speech" (pp. 40, 41). Two meanings of *aya* converge here: *aya* as "verse" [in the Qur'an] and *aya* as "sign," so that immersed in Qur'anic revelation, we come to regard things as signs of their creator. "The act of interpretation allows the human self to cross over ... from the visible to the hidden ... from the less real to the more real" (p. 47). Hence "the act of interpretation demands a constant enactment or 'performance' in the inner life of one who unlocks its meaning, [so] if the meaning of a verse in revelation is not contrary to reason, then we must accept the image as it is, as a manifestation of the Real" (p. 48). Ibn 'Arabi calls attention to *imagination* as the "*barzakh* or 'isthmus' ... from the sensible form to the invisible meaning" (p. 47) as an explicit antidote to the Islamic *falâsifa* (philosophers) who preceded him, notably Ibn Sina, whose quest for a "purely conceptual" mode of expression pretended to be better adapted to intelligible realities. Yet Ibn 'Arabi sought to give philosophic expression to a Muslim tradition which had elevated Qur'anic expression above "philosophy" for the way it employed images and similes designed to "take us by the hand" (*manuductio*) and lead us on the sublime realities.[20] In summary, for Ibn 'Arabi

> the goal is the complete assimilating of the self to the Word of God as revealed in the Qur'an ... through a thoroughly rigorous rational analysis of the text supplemented by a creative imagination that is able to go beyond rational categories to perceive the higher meanings intimated by the symbolic nature of the 'two books' of creation and the Qur'an. (p. 55)

And we could describe Meister Eckhart as engaged in a similar transformation of his predecessor, Thomas Aquinas, by insisting that *imagination* be a necessary ingredient in the ascent of the mind to God, even if *manuductio* is an apt description of Aquinas's own creative way of employing conceptual categories. And like Ibn 'Arabi, Eckhart focuses on Scripture as he

> attempts to show that philosophical categories ... attain the fullness of their truth-content only when understood in relation to the soul's ascent to and union with God [where] the soul is able to know these categories in their ideal origin, who is, of course, God.

Following Moses Maimonides, Eckhart is preoccupied with the standing gap between "multiple divine attributes [and] divine unity, and how it is possible for us humans to predicate accurately and adequately these attributes of God" (p. 62). For "as Aristotle demonstrated, all knowing is a unity of knower and known qua intelligible form, and if God is pure Intelligence, the knowledge of God would be absolute unity of knower and known" (p. 65). But given the palpable gap here, what is required "is to present reason's truths under the cover of parables or myths, so that it will stimulate the hearer to the activity of interpretation, and thus to an inward penetration of the divine mystery and the indwelling of the transcendent Truth" (p. 65). For Eckhart, "God as the transcendent cause of creation also corresponds to the immanent ground of the soul ... through the Incarnation of the Word" through whom all things are made (p. 68). So it becomes the "task of metaphysician [and] theologian [alike]: to make the divine *ratio* in and through which all beings are created transparent to reason insofar as this is possible" (p. 69). Yet it is "Scripture, insofar as it reveals the primal *ratio* or idea in which all things have been created, [that] contains within itself the key to knowing created beings in their divine ideas." So "the truths of metaphysics and even physics ... lies hidden under the 'husk' of images and parables of scripture" (p. 71).

In sum,

> Eckhart's entire intention ... is to reinsert the objective categories of speculative thought, whether in theology or in metaphysics, into

their origin and basis in the soul's living union with God in and through the divine Word or *ratio* and, by doing so, to transform this union from one of potentiality to actuality (p. 76), which will be effected only through "bringing forth the inner Word in loving detachment" (p. 78).

Yet it is crucial that this Word be incarnate so that "Christ performs the function analogous to that of the *mundus imaginalis* [in Ibn 'Arabi]: in his person materializ[ing] the spiritual and spiritualiz[ing] the material, [so becoming] the interpretive key not only to all of Scripture but to all creation" (p. 90). Thus Dobie's manner of comparing Islamic with Christian philosophical theology highlights the crucial parallel between the Qur'an and Jesus: where Christians believe that Jesus is the word of God made human, while Muslims believe that the Qur'an is the Word of God made book (Arabic). This strictly parallel presentation displays substantial differences as well, of course, allowing him to proceed so as to highlight similarity-in-difference. His concluding chapter on the venture of comparative study takes "these convergences as the implicit recognition by both Ibn 'Arabi and Meister Eckhart of the necessity for incorporating elements of other traditions into their own without compromising the orthodoxy of their traditions in any way" (p. 288). The key lies in the way each author's philosophical reflection is grounded in their respective revelational traditions, which Dobie goes on to trace in *existence*, *intellect*, and the *ideal human paradigm*, though our survey of *revelation* offers sufficient evidence of how this can be done when it is expertly executed.

Moses Maimonides: A Fresh Appreciation

The title of this section is more teasing than illuminating, for rather than offer a strict comparison between these two Jewish thinkers, pairing them will direct us to a fresh appraisal of Maimonides which reveals more of an affinity with Ibn 'Arabi and Meister Eckhart than with the "rationalist" title often given him. Here we also have two contemporary expositors, a generation apart, José Faur and Daniel Davies, each of whom exploits Maimonides' "dialectical" method of exposition to call our attention to realities "better *shown* than *said*" (Wittgenstein).[21] José Faur delineates, from a rabbinic perspective, the way that the Rambam employs reason to explore and to confirm revelation:

> In the Maimonidean system knowledge of God as a transcendent Supreme Being means knowledge of God as the absolute Creator. It involves three closely interrelated steps: exiting the realm of imagination, discovering objective reality, and cognizance of the Creator. The first step consists in freeing the mind from the grip of imagination. ... The second step consists of penetrating the realm of reason and perceiving reality as an objective entity governed by precise and universal laws. Only then can humans begin to realize that the universe in which they reside may be the design of a Creator, Absolute and Supreme. The source for this doctrine is rabbinic ... Only a mythological deity leaves traces of its presence. The God of Israel, even when performing the most astounding miracles, leaves no evidence of His presence (p. 13). ... In this fashion God, author of the universe, simultaneously bestows existence to the universe and covers His traces "out of existence."[22] The Maimonidean doctrine of Creation cannot be demonstrated: it can only be indicated (p. 14). ... [Yet] only a post-rational human can distinguish between what words *say* and what can only be pointed at but cannot be *said* (p. 15).

An entire program of philosophical theology is outlined here, culminating with resonances of Wittgenstein. The first step suggests that analogous uses of language will be indispensable, lest our imagination spontaneously infect statements intending to indicate the creator with inappropriate images. The second reminds us how using language analogously will presuppose a developed capacity for sensing an *order* which can never accurately be described (since it transcends imagining), while the third step – cognizance of the creator – takes us to the "post-rational" heart of the matter: "the realm of esoterics and prophecy" (p. 119).

Before following his lead to trace the Rambam's rich exercise program, however, we need to free Faur's image of *steps* "from the grip of imagination." The mention of "esoteric" offers an entry. As we have suggested, the polarity exoteric/esoteric can easily mislead us into thinking of the first as *literal*: "the Torah speaks in human language" as Maimonides never tired of reminding us, while the deliberately "contradictory premises" which he warns us will signal an invitation to "esoteric and prophetic" understanding will require *decoding*. But the very image of *decoding* presumes that intelligent persons will be able to transform scrambled language into something clear, thereby undercutting the signal difference in the third step: from saying to showing, from words to silence. As Faur puts it: "If one were to regard Creation as God's speech or writing – as the Scripture and rabbis teach – then a distinction must be established between what the system *says* and what it only *indicates*. [Creation] is structurally connected with the doctrine of silence" (p. 14). Yet if so, how can he go on to advise us how "to decode God's speech and writing?"[23] In fact, of course, much of the discussion of this exoteric/esoteric polarity has been infected with the *decoding* metaphor, which we shall have to ask the Rambam to help us excoriate, as a vestige of imaginal discourse, in order to be faithful to the path of interpretation which José Faur has opened for us. One way of beginning to do so is to remind ourselves (1) just how analogous are the notions of "God's *speech* and *writing*" in all of the Abrahamic faith-traditions, and (2) to use the deliberately ambiguous ladders of Sufi "stations" to explicate how the three *steps* which Faur proposes for articulating the Rambam's intellectual ascent from discourse to silence are not, of course, steps at all! That is, one never quite mounts from the first to the second and then to the third, since imagination will ever bedevil our notions, while we shall ever be tempted to project the orders which our intellect needs to understand into the source of order itself. Sufi writers take little care to be consistent in labeling the stations along the way to proximity with the divine, for there seems to be no single path, though a path will open for each, and it will be one of ascent, so *steps* or *stations* will prove to be useful metaphors so long as we realize that is what

they are. As the Rambam will suggest, that *realization* will distinguish a properly analogous use of language from one which simply relies on metaphors themselves to make the point.[24] And the very structure of the *Guide*, with its repetitive perambulations, is intended to prompt just such a realization.

So our minds, as human beings, will never be freed "from the grip of imagination," nor can our intellects ever claim to have grasped "objective reality." Indeed, with the help of our friends, we shall always be freeing whatever discourse we employ from unintended implications which imagination will spontaneously supply, just as we shall ever be directing our critical faculties to more adequate conceptualizations, as the history of science palpably reminds us.[25] We find this strategy operative in the *Guide* once its author moves beyond the foundational distinction of *knowledge* from *opinion*, roughly paralleling that of *reason* from *imagination*, to attempt to lead us into an appreciation of the ways revelation can enhance our understanding of matters which surpass demonstration – notably (as Faur identifies it) free creation. In short, we can learn to employ the very critical capacities we constantly need to move us beyond imagination, to help us ascend to a "post-rational" stance – though never without a guide, whose guidance will be displayed as we delineate the structure of his text: the *Guide of the Perplexed*.

Let me recall the suggestion of my initial guide in these matters, Joel Kraemer: that the *Guide* itself proceeds dialectically.[26] That is, *not* demonstratively, which is clearly the case. Yet if demonstration is the signature of *reason*, must that situate the *Guide* in the realm of *opinion*? Hardly, for then we would be entrusting ourselves to following what the Rambam says, rather than undertaking the exercises he has designed for us to do. A second meaning for "dialectical" can help resolve this apparent dilemma: a strategic amassing of examples to lead students to realize where the argument is headed; pedagogy, or *manudiuctio* ("taking by the hand and leading"), as Aquinas used it. .This constructive sense also responds to any reader's appreciation of the author of the *Guide* as an accomplished teacher. It is by virtue of such assembled examples that we are led to an ever more articulate way of expressing, say, how necessary emanation differs from free creation. Moreover, since the emanation scheme offers greater philosophical elegance, one will have to parse "free creation"' in such a way as to excoriate any Zeus-like willfulness from the action. Yet the action of free creating itself will escape positive articulation, since we cannot understand an action which is free yet does not alter the agent in effecting it. Nor are we able to parse activity which does not take place in time yet whose effect is temporal. So we are pressed to try as best we can to articulate who and what this agent is.

Here is where Maimonides' celebrated treatment of divine attributes emerges, for to safeguard the "distinction" between creator and creatures, he will insist that "God is One in every respect without plurality and without additions to His essence" (1.52).[27] Furthermore, he will deny any *relation* between creator and creatures, intending, of course, a reciprocal relation of the parent-child sort, best expressed in the Arabic custom of naming parents after their first son, so that the father becomes Abu Samir and the mother Umm Samir, though it is Samir who has come into the world through their agency. So what would it be like to have an agent who is in no way affected by its agency being operative? We can have recourse to Aristotle's teaching that the activity of the cause is in the effect, as the flame burns what is combustible without its being altered as a flame. Or we can give it a name, as Sara Grant does, using Shankara's *nonduality* to express creation in these traditions as a "non-reciprocal relation of dependence."[28] Yet while that offers a tidy formula, corresponding to Aquinas's insistence that while the relation of creatures to the creator is a *real* one, that of creator to creatures is not; both statements have evoked stiff objections: would not such a God be uncaring? Maimonides has a response, of course: *caring* cannot be said of God, for that would be adding something to the divinity, though one could certainly speak – as the Scriptures do – of God's actions as exhibiting caring. Yet those same scriptures often describe divine care in ways which would defy comparison with caring human actions. This further confirms the Rambam's insistence that we cannot "imagine a relation between a thing and

Him which shares no common trait with anything outside Him at all ... [So] there is no possible true relation between Him and anything He has created, because relation can at any time be only between things of the same immediate species. ... [Indeed,] how could there be any relation between God and any creature, when there is that immense difference in the nature of existence, greater than which no difference can ever be?" (1.52). But if the only relations we can imagine will be correlations, can we and do we not affirm a unique relation in naming God "creator?" And is not the divine activity of creating itself able to bridge that "immense difference?" The answer must be yes, of course, yet the Rambam has forcibly reminded us that we have no way of "tracking" such activity.

His way of showing this will be to offer different ways of presenting creation, where the differences in his presentation have led to fierce controversy over whether Maimonides held the universe to have been created such that it has an initial moment of existence or so that it has always existed. Sara Klein-Braslavy has laid out his consistent efforts to interpret the story in each of these ways without attempting to reconcile them.[29] Yet she goes on to conclude that such a strategy "shows that he wished to conceal his true view – namely, that the universe is eternal – from the common man."[30] But following the pedagogical dialectic of the *Guide*, there is no way of inferring Maimonides' "true view," that would be like asking Socrates what he really thinks! Yet if Socrates were to tell us what he "really thinks," we would be inclined to accept his opinion of things, when his goal – like the Rambam's – is to spur us on to think it out ourselves. Would it not be more in line with his intent, as manifested in the structure of the *Guide*, to read the dual presentation as a reminder that we have no way of suitably articulating in human speech the activity of creating, so are impelled to affirm of it what we must – that it is free – and allow for different – even conflicting – conceptual articulations? For at this point our speech can at best try to *show* what it realizes it cannot *say*. So any attempt to detect and convey "Maimonides' secret position on creation" will prove to be a vain search.[31]

The final chapters of the *Guide* intimate what this comes to, namely:

> the obligation of exercising one's independent power of thinking on the subject of God alone after having obtained the knowledge of Him. ... This is a form of service to God which is reserved for those who have apprehended Truth. The more they think about God and let their minds dwell upon Him, the more intensive their service to Him. (3.51)

Here we find a lead to José Faur's use of "post-rational" to characterize the goal of the Rambam's pedagogy: why else would one need to "exercise one's independent power of thinking ... *after* having obtained knowledge of the truth?" This is the transition from Faur's step two: "perceiving reality as an objective entity governed by precise and universal laws," to step three: "realizing that the universe in which they reside may be the design of a Creator, Absolute and Supreme." Moreover, that very "exercise of the mind" manifests itself as "a form of service to God ... reserved for those who have apprehended Truth." In the Islamicate, the Arabic term for "service" is interchangeable with that of "prayer," and in Maimonides' tradition, with fidelity to the Torah. The only way for the intellect to "grasp" what is beyond its grasp will be by way of altering one's life in the direction of the object sought; in this case, the One who is creator of all. After a particularly recondite exposition which leads beyond what can properly be said, the Rambam will often close the chapter by "ponder this well!" or in another rendering: "endeavor to understand this fully" (3.52). Or more fulsomely:

> Train yourself to understand this chapter, and make every effort to increase the number of occasions when you are with God or at least striving towards Him, and to diminish the occasions when you are with things other than He and not striving towards Him. This guidance is sufficient for the purpose of this treatise. (3.51 (Excursus))

How might we ponder things well, or endeavor to understand, or train ourselves to understand? As he himself suggests: be with

God or at least strive towards Him. The most obvious connection in Maimonides' cultural environment would be the Sufi practices of *recollection* (*dhikr*) leading to "closeness to God." Al-Ghazali details these in several places in his magnum opus, *Ihya' 'Ulum ad-Din* (with which most scholars think the Rambam had to be familiar), notably in the *Book of Faith in Divine Unity and Trust in Divine Providence* (*Kitab at-tawhid wa tawakkul*).[32] The structure of this book displays also its strategy: the first third treats of the foundational Islamic article of faith in the oneness of God; the last two-thirds on that quality of trust in this One God which testifies to our understanding of that foundational article, which defies a proper articulation. For Maimonides, "striving towards Him" will involve trusting in "that Divine Providence [which] is constantly guarding those who have obtained a share of that emanation which is granted to all who make an effort to obtain it. When persons have obtained purity of thought, clear perception of God by the proper methods, and beatitude through that which he perceives, it will never be possible for any evil of any kind to befall them, because they are with God and God is with them" (3.51). The "proper methods" for obtaining a "clear perception of God" will involve modes of service which lead to the grades of human perfection which he details in the culminating chapter (3.54). So we know that "perception" must be taken metaphorically (or analogously), and that it will not admit of the articulation proper to knowledge as we obtain it; it will, in short, be a "post-rational" sort of perception. That is, the intellectual mode may best describe it, but the manner of apprehension will exceed our intellectual powers as they are exercised in their best manner, in demonstration.[33]

Whatever it is, it will result from "that emanation which is granted to all who make an effort to obtain it," where the Rambam identifies the *emanation* with *prophecy*, and "prophecy" always refers, in the Islamicate, to the Scriptures in their power as the Word of God. And while our efforts are a *sine qua non*, prophecy can only be granted; it can never be an achievement. This suggests an affinity with Aquinas's celebrated response to the question whether "besides human reason, there is a further understanding which comes as a

119

result of grace?" He not only answers *yes*, but obliges with a lucid explanation of *how*: just as the deliverances of the senses are rendered intelligible when penetrated by the agent intellect, so the God-given images of Scripture (which he calls "prophetic visions") are illuminated by the intellect strengthened by grace to offer us an understanding greater than reason could yield (ST 1.12.13). So the "images of scripture," the literal sense of the (largely) narrative accounts, take the place of "deliverances of the senses," while the "light of grace" strengthens the agent intellect to yield the proper – that is, the God-given – sense of these "God-given images" (or "prophetic visions"). And while "grace" is a term Christians more easily employ, it would falsify the pervasive tone of these final chapters of the *Guide* were one to attempt to deny its efficacy in Maimonides.[34] What is of primary interest to us, however, is the manner of employing Scripture to enhance our properly human understanding of the universe itself, and especially in its relation to its creator. We need to learn how to let ourselves be guided by it, but if we may follow Aquinas's analogies, that guidance will be not unlike the guidance a teacher like Maimonides can offer in his *Guide*. God-given as it may be, its mode will follow the modes of understanding proper to us; we cannot expect any special illumination, but can nonetheless trust to God-given guidance.

A fine example of this is given in Maimonides' discussion in the *Mishneh Torah* of messianic times – an account which a Jerusalem student found exemplified a "rationalist" position on the matter. Without pretending to be an authority on intra-Jewish readings of the Rambam, I present this as clarifying confusions which can bedevil other communities as well. Famously, he teaches:

> Let no one think that in the days of the Messiah any of the laws of nature will be set aside, nor any innovation be introduced into creation. The world will follow its normal course. The words of Isaiah: "And the wolf shall dwell with the lamb, and the leopard lie down with the kid" (11:6) are to be understood figuratively, meaning that Israel will live securely among the wicked of the heathens who are likened to wolves and leopards, as it is written: "A wolf of the desert

does spoil them, a leopard watches over their cities" (Jer 5:6). They will all accept the true religion, and will neither plunder nor destroy, and together with Israel earn a comfortable living in a legitimate way, as it is written: "And the lion shall eat straw like the ox" (Isa. 11:7). All similar expressions used in connection with the Messianic age are metaphorical. In the days of King Messiah the full meaning of these metaphors and their allusions will become clear to all.[35]

In denying that "the laws of nature will be set aside," he may sound "rationalist" in the sense of eschewing any overt miracles, yet his insistence that "all will accept the true religion, and will neither plunder nor destroy, and together with Israel earn a comfortable living in a legitimate way," could hardly be presented as "natural" (or customary) comportment in the human world we all know! So the presence of "King Messiah" will clearly bring about transformations of a monumental sort, which no self-respecting "rationalist" would ever expect or soberly predict. Here again, it seems characteristic of what Maimonides will call "the imagination" to fancy the "supernatural" in overtly miraculous terms, while the Rambam himself has already reminded us of the utterly unlikely transformation which can be worked even in fractious times in "those who have obtained a share of that emanation which is granted to all who make an effort to obtain it ... it will never be possible for any evil of any kind to befall them, because they are with God and God is with them" (3.51). Not much "rationalism" in that description!

Before concluding, let us return to José Faur's third step: the heart of what he calls the "post-rational realm of esoterics and prophecy." This step can be likened to allowing the Scriptures of our traditions to guide our reflections, with a guidance which cannot promise an illumination beyond the ordinary, but will prove a reliable guide to properly weighing the factors affecting our understanding. In this way, we will learn to trust our Scriptures as leading us beyond what we could ourselves judge to be the case. Yet note that such guidance does not translate into a "secret position" or a "special insight" which we could formulate for anyone else. So it cannot rightly be called "knowledge" but those who trust in it can be called "post-rational." In this sense, the Scriptures, meditated and lived over a period of time, can provide a prescient context for the exercise of reason in inquiry, and so rightly be called a "grace" Faithful followers of revelation can enter, then, "the realm of esoterics and prophecy," by allowing themselves to trust the guidance given them by revelation as it is received and elaborated in the community it forms.

Now as José Faur has suggested (and persuasively documented) a fresh way of reading the Rambam, notably by showing us how the passage to the esoteric is already inscribed in our shared faith (as Abrahamic believers) in the free creation of the universe, we have already witnessed a similar dynamic in Ibn 'Arabi and of Meister Eckhart. And with the same point of contention which José Faur identifies in Maimonides: the ineffable relation of creator to creatures, as well as of creatures to the creator. (For these are not reciprocal, as Maimonides presumed they had to be, yet Aquinas famously denied: a difference which Sara Grant articulates adroitly with Shankara's help.) Moreover, it was precisely the way both Meister Eckhart and Ibn 'Arabi struggled to portray the uniqueness of this relation which made them suspect to their respective communities: Eckhart was publicly tried by ecclesiastical authorities for preaching pantheism, and Ibn 'Arabi continues to be banned in portions of the Arab Muslim world (including, until recently, Egypt) for his famous (or notorious) teaching of *wahdat al-wujud*, or "unity of existence" between creatures and their creator. Yet again, neither of them denies that creator and creatures are distinct from one another, yet both struggle to articulate how utterly unique that *distinction* must be: that it cannot be at all parallel with the distinctions we draw among creatures. The Rambam's strategy for avoiding a pantheism which effectively denies free creation by eliding any distinction at all between origin and result was to deny any relation at all between creatures and creator. But that only succeeds in underscoring the "distinction" by making talk of creation itself incoherent, for asserting that all things are freely created by one God clearly requires the unique relation of creating; the trick lies in articulating it. His wholesale denial may well have expressed a heroic attempt to avoid falling into the trap of trying to imagine an ineffable relation, given the ubiquitous power images inevitably have in shaping our attempts to articulate these recondite matters.

We have seen how Ibn 'Arabi and Eckhart countered this propensity by proposing pregnant alternative metaphors, designed to divert the conventional powers of imaging by offering arresting counter-images. In doing so, they each displayed their respect for the Rambam's concerns about religious thinkers unwittingly promoting idolatry, and were predictably rewarded for their efforts by religious authorities finding them suspect as well. What to do? Very little, it seems, about religious authorities, yet José Faur has shown us how the Rambam offers a way to wean inquirers away from their spontaneous proposals by showing how contradictory they can be. In this way we are returned to revelation itself, so helping us to recognize when revelation itself directs us *not* to take its assertions at face value. It rather directs our minds and hearts to a teaching which defies straightforward articulation, however overtly it may assert the free creation of the universe!

The initial challenge will be to recognize those moments, while the next one will be to resist the offer of someone to decode them for us, thereby promising to clarify what Scripture itself leaves obscure. Yet both these thinkers join the Rambam to insist that neither obscurity nor idolatrous pretension to know need be the last word. For we can let ourselves be guided by the liminal moments in encountering our revelations to respond with a willing heart, letting obscurity lead us to give witness to the truth which emerges from our puzzlement. Then we will have learned how to apprentice our powers of reasoning to a revelation which can shape both our understanding and our lives, as we allow the power inherent in that revealing activity to be made manifest in thought and in action. In this way the dynamics of "return" are articulated and practiced, as we have witnessed in Jewish, Christian, and Muslim traditions whose distinct pathways can nonetheless display remarkable convergences from our privileged perspective. In the following chapter we shall encounter living witnesses who have traversed those pathways in each tradition.

123

Notes

1 Peter Hawkins, *Undiscovered Country* (New York: Seabury, 2009).
2 Sadr al-Din al-Shirazi (Mulla Sadra), *The Divine Manifestations of the Secrets of the Perfecting Sciences* (trans. and annotated Fazel Asadi Amjad, Mahdi Dasht Bozorgi; London: Institute of Ismaili Studies, 2010).
3 Marcia Hermansen, "Eschatology," in Tim Winter (ed.), *Cambridge Companion to Classical Islamic Theology* (Cambridge: Cambridge University Press, 2008), pp. 308–322.
4 Mulla Sadra Shirazi, *Spiritual Psychology: The Fourth Intellectual Journey in Transcendent Philosophy*, Volumes VIII and IX of *the Asfar* (translated, introduced and annotated by Latimah-Parvin Peerwani; London: ICAS Press, 2008), pp. 669–670, citing Ibn 'Arabi: *Futûhât al-Makkiyya*.
5 Jon Levenson, *Creation and the Persistence of Evil: The Jewish Drama of Divine Omnipotence* (Princeton, NJ: Princeton University Press, 1994); John Milbank, *Theology and Social Theory* (Oxford: Blackwell, 1992); David Burrell and Elena Malits, *Original Peace: Restoring God's Creation* (New York: Paulist Press, 1997).
6 Letter of Pope St. Clement to the Corinthians, 38.1–2, 4, in Maxwell Staniforth (ed.), *Early Christian Writings* (Harmondsworth: Penguin Classics, 1968).
7 *Sancti Columbani Opera*, trans. Walker: *Instructio* 11.1–2 (Dublin: Institute of Advanced Studies, n.d.).
8 Portions of the following have been adapted from my "Faith as a Way of Knowing in John of the Cross and Edith Stein," in Martin Boler and Anthony Cernera (eds), *The Contribution of Monastic Life to the Church and the World* (Fairfield, CT: Sacred Heart University Press, 2006), pp. 167–179.
9 Edith Stein, *Self-portrait in Letters* (Washington DC: Institute of Carmelite Studies, 1993).
10 John of the Cross, *The Spiritual Canticle, The Living Flame of Love* in *Collected Works of St. John of the Cross* (Washington DC: Institute of Carmelite Studies, 1991).
11 Edith Stein, *Science of the Cross* (trans. Hilda Graef; Chicago: Regnery, 1960), p. xxi.
12 *Analogia entis: Metaphysik* (Einsedeln, 1962); Cornelio Fabro, *Participation et causalité selon S. Thomas d'Aquin* (Paris: Nauwelaerts, 1961); Louis

Geiger, *La participation dans la philosophie de S. Thomas d'Aquin* (Paris: J. Vrin, 1953).

13   *Endliches und Ewiges Sein* (Leuven: Nauwelaerts / Freiburg: Herder, 1950), p. viii.

14   Stein, *Self-portrait in Letters*, Section 29a.

15   Stein, *Self-portrait in Letters*, Section 149.

16   See Peter M. Candler, Jr, *Theology, Rhetoric, Manuductio* or *Reading Scripture Together on the Path to God* (Grand Rapids, MI; Cambridge, UK: Eerdmans, 2006).

17   *Endliches und Ewiges Sein* (Leuven: Nauwelaerts; Freiburg: Herder, 1950), pp. 320–321.

18   See, among others, Robert Dobie, *Logos and Revelation: Ibn 'Arabi, Meister Eckhart, and Mystical Hermeneutics* (Washington DC: Catholic University of America Press, 2010); Reza Shah-Kazemi, *Paths to Transcendence according to Shankara, Ibn Arabi and Meister Eckhart* (Bloomington, IN: World Wisdom Books, 2006; French translation, *Shankara, Ibn 'Arabi et Maître Eckhart: La Voie de la Transcendance* (Paris: L'Harmatta, 2010); and Ghasem Kakaie: "The extrovertive Unity of Existence from Ibn 'Arabi's and Meister Eckhart's Viewpoints," *Topoi* 26 (2007), 177–189; "Ibn Arabi's God, Eckhart's God: Philosophers' God or Religion's God?" in Norbert Hintersteiner (ed.), *Naming and Thinking God in Europe, Today Theology in Global Dialogue* (Amsterdam; New York: Rodopi, 2007), pp. 411–427; "Interreligious Dialogue, Ibn Arabi and Meister Eckhart," *Journal of the Mhuhyiddin 'Arabi Society* 45 (2009), 45–63.

19   See my *Knowing the Unknowable God: Ibn Sina, Maimonides, Aquinas* (Notre Dame, IN: University of Notre Dame Press, 1986); and my "Act of Creation with its Theological Consequences," in David Burrell, Carlo Cogliati, and Janet Soskice (eds), *Creation and the God of Abraham* (Cambridge: Cambridge University Press, 2010).

20   See Salman H. Bashier, *Ibn al-'Arabi's Barzakh: Concept of the Limit and the Relationship between God and the World* (Albany: State University of New York Press, 2004).

21   References to José Faur follow; I can alert readers to Daniel Davies's work to be published (in 2011) by Oxford University Press: *Method and Metaphysics in Maimonides' Guide* (Reflection and Theory in the Study of Religion Series). Davies reads the *Guide of the Perplexed* with a judicious and philosophically trained mind. Adopting Joel Kraemer's insistence that the *Guide* is a dialectical treatise, he defends

the propriety of dialectical reasoning in this domain where little (if anything) can be known properly. Moreover, by accepting the adequacy of dialectical reasoning in such matters, he is able to sidestep various hypotheses regarding "hidden readings." Employing the philosophical strategies of Barry Miller to elucidate the uniqueness of the relation of creator to creatures, Davies can show why his assertions can only be of a dialectical sort, yet in that sense can also be read straightforwardly: to show that it is possible to speak of the creator as a being whose very essence is to-be, yet do so without falling into oxymoronic consequences.

22 José Faur directs us to his article: "God as Writer: Omnipresence and the Art of Dissimulation," *Cross Currents* 6 (1989), 37–38, but see especially *Homo mysticus: A Guide to Maimonides's Guide for the Perplexed* (Syracuse, NY: Syracuse University Press, 1998), and for context, his earlier *Golden Doves with Silver Dots: Semiotics and Textuality in Rabbinic Tradition* (Bloomington, IN: Indiana University Press, 1986).

23 His advice is explicitly incoherent, which suggests that he realized how misleading is the decoding metaphor: "to decode God's speech and writing, the hearer/reader must fill in the intervals between the letters and the words, discovering the syntax which is manifested but not located in them, like Bezalel, the builder of the tabernacle, who 'knew' how to join the letters by which Heaven and earth were created. Thus 'proving' Creation is the same kind of oxymoron as a proposition articulating the syntax of its own syntax" (p. 14). See also Catherine Pickstock, *After Writing* (Oxford: Blackwell, 2001).

24 Many have difficulty distinguishing *analogy* from *metaphor* because they expect the words themselves to differ; it is the realization, the use itself, which turns the trick.

25 Bas van Fraasen's *Empirical Stance* (New Haven, CT: Yale University Press, 2002) develops this latter point elegantly.

26 See his magisterial study: *Maimonides: The Life and World of One of Civilization's Greatest Minds* (New York: Doubleday, 2008).

27 For a contemporary approach, see Robert Sokolowski, *The God of Faith and Reason* (Washington DC: Catholic University of America Press, 1992), who uses his phenomenological skills to elucidate what he calls "the distinction" of creator from creation. To find analogs in Jewish and Muslim tradition, see my "The Christian Distinction Celebrated and Expanded," in John Drummond and James Hart (eds),

The Truthful and the Good (Dordrecht: Kluwer Academic Publishers, 1996), pp. 191–206.

28 Sara Grant, *Towards an Alternative Theology* (Notre Dame, IN: University of Notre Dame Press, 2002).

29 *Perush ha-Rambam le-Sippu Beri' at ha-'Olam* (Jerusalem, 1978), cited in Aviezer Ravitsky, "The Secrets of the *Guide to the Perplexed*: Between the Thirteenth and the Twentieth Centuries," in Isadore Twersky (ed.), *Studies in Maimonides* (Cambridge, MA: Harvard University Press, 1990), pp. 159–207, citation at p. 193.

30 *Perush*, p. 256.

31 Herbert Davidson, "Maimonides' Secret Position on Creation," in Isidore Twersky (ed.), *Studies in Medieval Jewish History and Literature I* (Cambridge, MA: Harvard University Press, 1979), pp. 15–19.

32 Al-Ghazali, *Book of Faith in Divine Unity and Trust in Divine Providence (Kitab at-tawhid wa tawakkul)* (trans. David Burrell; Louisville: Fons Vitae, 2002).

33 Schlomo Pines has explored this in an article which places the Rambam firmly in the Islamicate, "The Limitations of Human Knowledge according to al-Farabi, ibn Bajja, and Maimonides," in Isidore Twersky (ed.), *Studies in Medieval Jewish History and Literature I* (Cambridge, MA: Harvard University Press, 1979), pp. 83–109.

34 See Avital Wohlman's presentation of Yesheyahu Leibowitz's views, in her *Maimonide et Thomas d'Aquin: Un Dialogue Impossible* (Fribourg: Presses Universitaires, 1999).

35 *Mishneh Torah* 14.12.1, in Isadore Twersky (ed.), *A Maimonides Reader* (New York, Berhman House, 1972), p. 224; see also *Guide* 2.29.

6

Realized Eschatology: Faith as a Mode of Knowing and Journeying

A goal boldly affirmed yet bereft of commensurately bold descriptions can only provoke skepticism: how can we know it is true? And when that goal envisages all of mankind as well as each human person, together with the universe which sustains all living things, the ensuing skepticism will range universally as well. How can claims so cosmic ever be corroborated? The response each Abrahamic faith proposes will display a common pattern: the shape of the goal will be limned in the ways delineated to attain it. The life of faith becomes a pilgrimage towards the absent goal, which remains obscure yet attracts by offering a way forward. In this way, a set of practices – "spiritual exercises" – can intimate a presence-in-absence whose very absence may indeed serve to confirm the goal as an illusion, or whose hidden presence may gradually exercise an unmistakable attraction. So it seems inevitable that each of these traditions, but especially Christianity and Islam which project dramatic end-time scenarios, would have to find ways of incorporating the attraction of that goal into a trajectory leading to it. Jews have

Towards a Jewish-Christian-Muslim Theology, First Edition. David B. Burrell.
© 2011 John Wiley & Sons Ltd. Published 2011 by John Wiley & Sons Ltd.

been given the archetypal path of exodus from slavery, with Torah for a guide, a path which Christians adapted to structure Jesus' invitation to follow him in repentance, while Muslims are offered the call as well as the demand of pilgrimage. So while each Abrahamic faith may be focused on its goal, what gives each a distinctive structure is the way it offers to attain that goal.

This chapter will focus on the ways each Abrahamic tradition offers to attain its transcendent goal, noting fruitful crossovers among them. Yet as the image of pilgrimage reveals, such paths are never solitary, but replete with encounters among the pilgrims. In the spirit of this inquiry, we have no difficulty imagining a pilgrimage among Abrahamic believers in the new world into which we have been introduced. So while each path remains distinct, wayfarers formed in distinctive ways can encounter one another, offering each other assistance along the way. This mutual hospitality, dramatized in Chaucer's *Canterbury Tales*, enhances the paths themselves, as bearers of each tradition come to appreciate what others bring to them, incorporating that contribution into their respective lives. And in fact, some form of mutual exchange has stamped each tradition whenever exchange did occur, offering illuminating precedents for the world in which we now live. Those profiting from such fruitful exchange became "border-crossers" who exemplified in their lives and work the "creative hermeneutics" this inquiry tries to delineate and celebrate. Invariably thrust into a prophetic role, they exemplify (at their best) fresh and fertile reaches of their respective traditions, straining to direct those traditions towards their goal by allowing differences, as well as similarities, to further clarify that goal.

Exhibit 1: Mohandas Gandhi

Indeed, the primary example of such fruitful exchange for our century is Mohandas Gandhi, whose distance from the Abrahamic traditions, together with a distinctive relation to them via Tolstoy, has endowed him with a peculiar authority for our time. For he proved able to challenge each of those traditions for the ways they had allowed power to alienate themselves from their own revelational sources, all in the name of a complacent colonialism which made that inner betrayal all the more evident. (Our final chapter will sharply delineate the lamentable legacy of racism and terror which accompanied colonialist expansion, often enough legitimizing it in the name of one of these religious traditions.[1]) So Gandhi's provenance from the Asian subcontinent under the *raj*, together with his early professional life as an Indian expatriate serving as a barrister in British South Africa, gave him a formation well adapted to become a colonial collaborator or one required of a freedom-fighter. What made him take one path rather than the other is what interests us, so we let him delineate the distinctive way in which he undertook the struggle for freedom from a colonial yoke.

Urged by others to write his story, he presents it as "the story of my numerous experiments with truth." Yet "as my life consists of nothing but those experiments, it is true that the story will take the shape of an autobiography." Yet one goal directs all: "What I want to achieve – what I have been striving and pining to achieve these thirty years, – is self-realization, to see God face to face, to attain *moksha*. I live and move and have my being in pursuit of this goal. All that I do by way of speaking and writing, and all my ventures in the political field, are directed to this same end." Yet "there can be no room for self-praise. They can only add to my humility. The more I reflect and look back on the past, the more vividly do I feel my limitations." Yet the goal prevails: "to see the universal and all-pervading Spirit of Truth face to face one must be able to love the meanest of creation as oneself. And a man who aspires after that cannot afford to keep out of any field of life. That is why my devotion to Truth has drawn me into the field of politics; and I can say without the slightest hesitation, and yet in all humility, that those who say that religion has nothing to do with politics do not know what religion means." So far "the experiences and experiments have sustained me and given me great joy. But I know that I have still before me a difficult path to traverse. I must reduce myself to zero. So long as a man does not of his own free will put himself last among his fellow creatures, there is no salvation for him. *Ahimsa* is the farthest limit of humility."

True to his tradition, Gandhi recalls his origins and the source of his convictions.

My father was a lover of his clan, truthful, brave and generous ... he was incorruptible and had earned a name for strict impartiality in his family as well as outside. ... [He] never had any ambition to accumulate riches and left us very little property. He had no education, save that of experience ... but his rich experience of practical affairs stood him in good stead in the solution of the most intricate questions and in managing hundreds of men. Of religious training he had very little, but ... in his last days he began reading the *Gita* at the instance of a learned Brahman friend of the family, and he used to repeat aloud some verses every day at the time of worship. ... The outstanding impression my mother has left on my memory is that of saintliness. She was deeply religious. She would not think of taking her meals without her daily prayers. ... She would take the hardest vows and keep them without flinching. Illness was no excuse for relaxing them. I can recall her once falling ill when she was observing the *Chandrayana* vow, but the illness was not allowed to interrupt the observance.

So the politics to which he was drawn and seeks to implement can only be guided by *truth* – and as he is given to see it while he moves towards it: "for me, truth is the sovereign principle, which includes numerous other principles. This truth is not only truthfulness in word, but truthfulness in thought also, and not only the relative truth of our conception, but the Absolute Truth, the Eternal Principle, that is God." Yet though "I worship God as Truth only. I have not yet found Him, but I am seeking after Him. I am prepared to sacrifice the things dearest to me in pursuit of this quest. Even if the sacrifice demanded be my very life." Yet "as long as I have not realized this Absolute Truth, so long must I hold by the relative truth as I have conceived it. That relative truth must, meanwhile, be my beacon, my shield and buckler." Yet these remain relative to "the Absolute Truth," of which "in my progress I have had faint glimpses, God, and daily the conviction is growing upon me that He alone is real and all else is unreal." So his story is more than a story; it is an invitation: "let those, who wish, realize how the conviction has grown upon me; let them share my experiments and share also my conviction if they can. ... The instruments for the quest of truth are as simple as they are difficult. They may appear quite impossible to an arrogant person, and quite possible to an innocent child. The seeker after truth should be humbler than the dust."

Now the drawing power of this same truth – aspired to as well as realized piecemeal – conveyed the strength needed to confront raw power in Punjab: "as I proceeded further and further with my inquiry into the atrocities that had been committed on the people, I came across tales of government tyranny and the arbitrary despotism of its officers such as I was hardly prepared for, and they filled me with deep pain. ... The task of drafting the report of this Committee was also entrusted to me. I would recommend a perusal of this report to any one who wants to have an idea of the kind of atrocities that were perpetrated on the Punjab people." Moreover, "there is not a single conscious exaggeration in it anywhere, and every statement made in it is substantiated by evidence. Moreover, the evidence published was only a fraction of what was in the Committee's possession. ... This report, prepared as it was solely with a view to bringing out the truth and nothing but the truth, will enable the reader to see to what lengths the British Government is capable of going, and what inhumanities and barbarities it is capable of perpetrating in order to maintain its power. So far as I am aware, not a single statement made in this report has ever been disproved."

In signing off this modest appraisal of his life and work, he reiterates its goal: "I set a high value on my experiments. I do not know whether I have been able to do justice to them. I can only say that I have spared no pains to give a faithful narrative. To describe truth, as it has appeared to me, and in the exact manner in which I have arrived at it, has been my ceaseless effort. The exercise has given me ineffable mental peace, because, it has been my fond hope that it might bring faith in Truth and *Ahimsa* to waverers." Yet this sketch of a life-story only hints at the secret bonding of "the relative truth of our conception [with] the Absolute Truth, the Eternal Principle, that is God." That bond is revealed in the indissoluble link between means and ends that marked Gandhi's practice: a just polity can never be realized by unjust means. This grasp of the "goods internal to practice" links Gandhi's with Alasdair MacIntyre's reading of Aristotle's politics, in stark contrast to the external, instrumental relation between means and ends which dominated utilitarian political theory and practice, offering meretricious cover for the raw colonial power play which Gandhi witnessed so poignantly in Punjab and experienced all his life. Indeed, the only response he was able to make to a query about "Western civilization" was that "it would be a good idea."

As Charles Taylor astutely delineates in his monumental *A Secular Age*, the reductive deism that prevailed in Britain at the time let "religion" to be co-opted to offer flimsy justification of the power to exploit vast regions of humanity, effectively negating the Christian doctrine of one creator and a single humanity.[2] Colonialism proved to be the lethal cutting edge of the touted "enlightenment," abetted by a political ideology which severed means from ends, so that goals could float free from practice to offer pious "justification" of ostensibly "unavoidable policies" carried out in the service of the stated goals but often starkly at variance from them. Gandhi saw clearly that allowing oneself to be caught in that incoherent game would amount to a betrayal of authentic politics, so directed a nation seeking freedom from colonialism to steel itself to confront the lethal edge of dominating power with a radically different political philosophy – *ahimsa* – whose secret truth lay in never separating means from ends or ends from means.

Similarly, eschewing the ever-present temptation to separate his own experience from that of his exploited people brought him a clear diagnosis of the way "Western civilization" was internally linked with the brutalities of colonialism, in stark contrast with the only means which could bring true freedom to his people. *Ahimsa* represents an experimental approach to developing and implementing an authentic political philosophy in the face of the raw power of ideology. Gandhi never deserted the frontlines in his search for humane political truth. Moreover, the way he integrates theory with practice offers a stark challenge to the Abrahamic faiths, though the explicit inspiration of Tolstoy on his development could well suggest that his invocation of Hindu (or Jain) traditions already represented a transformation of that ethos.

How traditions develop

What history has shown is that the presence of other-believers can help faithful in each tradition to gain insight into the distortions of that tradition: the ways it has compromised with seductions of state power, or ways in which fixation on a particular *other* effectively skewed their understanding of the revelation given them. Minority voices within a tradition can often help make that clear, as Mennonites trace compromising elements in Western Christianity to an early alliance with Constantine, while Sufi Muslims remind their Sunni and Shi'a companions in faith of the crippling effects of a soul-less *shar'ia*, harkening to the way religious and secular leaders colluded in Baghdad in 922 to dispose of Ibn Mansur al-Hallaj: "his hands and his feet were cut off, he was hanged on the gallows, and then decapitated; his body was burned and its ashes cast into the Tigris."[3] Indeed, the memory of his martyrdom continues to haunt the Islamic world as a poignant reminder of God's presence among us in holy men and women. In fact, this towering figure became the inner guide of Louis Massignon, the French Islamicist whose life spanned the first two-thirds of the twentieth century, guiding his return to his Catholicism in a way which allowed him to continue to be instructed by the vibrant faith of his Muslim friends.[4] His friendship with Paul VI also allowed his voice to resonate in the way that *Nostra Aetate* directed Catholics to a fresh appreciation of Islam. Indeed, each of the twentieth-century figures who stand out as spiritual leaders in their respective traditions reflects a creative interaction with another faith-tradition, from Martin Buber and Franz Rosenzweig in Judaism, to Louis Massignon, Jules Monchanin, and Bede Griffiths among Catholic Christians; and in Islam, the Pathan leader and man of God, 'Abdul Ghaffar Khan, who responded to the inspiration of Gandhi to form a hundred thousand Pathan nonviolent soldiers, to help bring independence to India.

Exhibit 2: "A Man to Match his Mountains"

The life and work of Gandhi's Pathan counterpart, 'Abdul Ghaffar Khan, has been detailed by Eknath Easwaran in a biography appropriately entitled *A Man to Match his Mountains* (1984), followed by a documentary, entitled "The Frontier Gandhi: Badshah Khan, a Torch for Peace," by T.C. McLuhan, which received the 2009 award for *Best Documentary Film* at the Middle East International Film Festival. Ghaffar Khan was born into a generally peaceful and prosperous family from Charsadda, in the Peshawar Valley of British India. His father, Behram Khan was a local farmer in Charsadda. Ghaffar was the second son of Behram to attend the British-run Edward's mission school – an unusual arrangement since it was discouraged by the local mullahs. At school the young Ghaffar did well in his studies and was inspired by his mentor Reverend Wigram to see the importance of education in service to the community. In his tenth and final year of high school he was offered a highly prestigious commission in The Guides, an elite corps of Pashtun soldiers of the British Raj. Ghaffar refused the commission after realizing even Guide officers were still second-class citizens in their own country. He resumed his intention of university study and Reverend Wigram offered him the opportunity to follow his brother, Khan Sahib, to study in London. While he eventually received the permission of his father, Ghaffar's mother was not willing to lose another son to London, and perhaps to their own culture and religion as the mullahs warned her. So Ghaffar began working on his father's lands while attempting to discern what more he might do with his life.

In response to his inability to continue his own education, Ghaffar Khan turned to helping others start theirs. Like many such regions of the world, the strategic importance of the newly formed North-

West Frontier Province (NWFP) as a buffer for the British Raj from Russian influence was of little benefit to its residents. The oppression of the British, the repression of the mullahs, and an ancient culture of violence and vendetta prompted Ghaffar to want to serve and uplift his fellow men and women by means of education. At 20 years of age, Ghaffar opened his first school in Utmanzai. It was an instant success and he was soon invited into a larger circle of progressively minded reformers. While he faced much opposition and personal difficulties, Ghaffar Khan worked tirelessly to organize and raise the consciousness of his fellow Pushtuns. Between 1915 and 1918 he visited every one of the 500 settled districts of the Frontier. It was in this frenzied activity that he had come to be known as *Badshah (Bacha) Khan* (King of Chiefs).

In time, Ghaffar Khan's goal came to be the formulation of a united, independent, secular India. To achieve this end, he founded the *Khudai Khidmatgar* ("Servants of God"), commonly known as the "Red Shirts" (*Surkh Posh*), during the 1920s. The *Khudai Khidmatgar* was founded on a belief in the power of Gandhi's notion of *Satyagraha*, a form of active nonviolence as captured in an oath. He told its members: "I am going to give you such a weapon that the police and the army will not be able to stand against it. It is the weapon of the Prophet, but you are not aware of it. That weapon is patience and righteousness. No power on earth can stand against it." The organization recruited over 100,000 members and became legendary in opposing (and dying at the hands of) the British-controlled police and army. Through strikes, political organization, and nonviolent opposition, the *Khudai Khidmatgar* were able to achieve some success and came to dominate the politics of the NWFP. His brother, Dr Khan Abdul Jabbar Khan (known as Dr Khan Sahib), led the political wing of the movement, and was the Chief Minister of the province, from the late 1920s until 1947 when his government was dismissed by Mohammad Ali Jinnah of the Muslim League.

Ghaffar Khan had forged a close, spiritual, and uninhibited friendship with Mohandas (Mahatma) Gandhi, the pioneer of nonviolent mass civil disobedience in India. The two had a deep admiration towards each other and worked together closely till 1947. The *Khudai Khidmatgar* (Servants of God) agitated and worked cohesively with the Indian National Congress, the leading national organization fighting for freedom, of which Ghaffar Khan was a senior and respected member. On several occasions when the Congress seemed to disagree with Gandhi on policy, Ghaffar Khan remained his staunchest ally. In 1931 the Congress offered him the presidency of the party, but he refused, saying: "I am a simple soldier and Khudai Khidmatgar, and I only want to serve." (He remained a member of the Congress Working Committee for many years, resigning only in 1939 because of his differences with the Party's War Policy. He rejoined the Congress Party when the War Policy was revised.) On April 23, 1930, Ghaffar Khan was arrested during protests arising out of the Salt Satyagraha. A crowd of Khudai Khidmatgar gathered in Peshawar's Kissa Khwani (Storytellers) Bazaar. The British ordered troops to open fire with machine guns on the unarmed crowd, killing an estimated 200–250. The Khudai Khidmatgar members acted in accord with their training in nonviolence under Ghaffar Khan, facing bullets as the troops fired on them.

In the wake of the 1947 partition of India, Ghaffar Khan took the oath of allegiance to the new nation of Pakistan on February 23, 1948 at the first session of the Pakistan Constituent Assembly. He pledged full support to the government and attempted to reconcile with the founder of the new state Muhammad Ali Jinnah. Initial overtures led to a successful meeting in Karachi; however, a follow-up meeting in the Khudai Khidmatgar headquarters never materialized. So Ghaffar Khan formed Pakistan's first national opposition party on May 8, 1948 – the Pakistan Azad Party. The Party pledged to play the role of constructive opposition and be non-communal in its philosophy. However, suspicions of his allegiance persisted, and under the new Pakistani government Ghaffar Khan was placed under house arrest without charge from 1948 till 1954. Released from prison, he gave a speech again on the floor of the constituent assembly, this time condemning the massacre of his supporters at Babrra: "I had to go to prison many a time in the days of the

Britishers. Although we were at loggerheads with them, yet their treatment was to some extent tolerant and polite. But the treatment which was meted out to me in this Islamic state of ours was such that I would not even like to mention it to you."

Arrested several times between late 1948 and in 1956, the government attempted in 1958 to reconcile with him and offered him a ministry in the government. But after the assassination of his brother, he refused. He remained in prison till 1957 only to be re-arrested in 1958 until an illness in 1964 allowed for his release. From 1972 to 1980 Ghaffar Khan was arrested several times during the government of Zulfikar Ali Bhutto and the next military government, spending 52 years of his life imprisoned or in exile. Dying in Peshawar under house arrest in 1988, he was buried in Jalalabad in Afghanistan, according to his wishes. This symbolic move by Ghaffar Khan would allow his dream of Pashtun unification to live even after his death. The Indian government declared a five-day period of mourning in his honor. Although he had been repeatedly imprisoned and persecuted, tens of thousands of mourners attended his funeral, marching through the historic Khyber Pass from Peshawar to Jalalabad. A cease-fire was announced in the Afghan civil war to allow the funeral to take place.

Ghaffar Khan was a champion of women's rights and nonviolence. He became a hero in a society dominated by violence; notwithstanding his liberal views, his unswerving faith and obvious bravery led to immense respect. Throughout his life, he never lost faith in his nonviolent methods or in the compatibility of Islam and nonviolence. He viewed his struggle as a *jihad*, with only the enemy holding swords. He was closely identified with Gandhi because of his nonviolence principles and he is known in India as the "Frontier Gandhi." While the fledgling state of Pakistan, led by mullahs and military men, could hardly countenance Badshah Kahn, imprisoning him and systematically suppressing his army of Khudai Khidmatgars, a recent assessment of Pakistan by William Dalrymple notes how the movement has "made a dramatic comeback under the leadership of Ghaffar Khan's grandson, Asfandyar Wali Khan."[5] So even when religious and political leaders unite to reject the challenge of voices proposing renewal, those voices can also re-emerge.

Exhibit 3: A Jewish Awakening during Occupation in World War II Holland[6]

Let us focus next on Etty Hillesum, whose *Interrupted Life* was celebrated in the *New York Review of Books* as a "masterpiece of spirituality," a term one might not have expected in that sophisticated literary journal. These diaries first appeared in English in 1985, after painstaking efforts to render this account, composed under the crabbed conditions of Nazi occupation, into legible Dutch. Combined later with her "letters from Westerbork" into a single edition (1996), the extended narrative offers an intimate account of spiritual awakening on the part of an expressly bohemian, hence "secular," Jew, in the face of imminent extermination.[7] These spontaneously reflective entries document a person seeking to center and order her life, who one day finds herself "forced to the ground by something stronger than myself. … I suddenly went down on my knees in the middle of this large room … almost automatically" (p. 76). And the consequences of that action, in the context of her interaction with Julius Spier, her psychoanalyst and intimate friend, led her inner life to unfold to the point where she can say – in the midst of the misery of Westerbork, a staging area for transport to Auschwitz – "time and again it soars straight from my heart – I can't help it, that's just the way it is, like some elementary force – the feeling that life is glorious and magnificent" (p. 247). Nor is that feeling ephemeral, but a power making her over from within: "[as] the threat grows ever greater, and terror increases from day to day, I draw prayer round me like a dark protective wall, … and then step outside again, calmer and stronger …" (p. 139). "It always spreads from the inside outwards with me …" (p. 146). This courage is displayed by one who confesses: "I have never been able to 'do' anything; I can only let things take their course and if need be suffer" (p. 249). An apt remark from a woman who sought therapy shortly after her twenty-seventh birthday, sensing a void in herself and her relationships: "I am … just about seasoned enough I should think to be counted among the better lovers, and love does indeed suit me to perfection, and yet … deep inside me something is still locked away" (p. 1).

So runs the opening paragraph of her diaries, plausibly the task given her by the man whom she had sought out, Julius Spier, as a catalyst to their inner work. What follows can usefully be divided into three roughly even parts: her discovery of herself through the relationship with Spier which ensues (pp. 1–82), a period of preparation for serving others (pp. 82–160), and the actual crafting of her life as gift (pp. 160–243). The final phase begins at the point where all illusions are torn away: "What is at stake is our impending destruction and annihilation" (p. 160), and is focused by the death of the guide whom she had come to love: "You taught me to speak the name of God without embarrassment. You were the mediator … and now … my path leads straight to God. … And I shall be the mediator for any other soul I can reach" (pp. 209–210).

These remarks were written after she had volunteered to accompany the first group of Jews being sent to Westerbork. Yet they are rooted in the second, preparatory phase, as she discovers, encountering a former lover, that "everything is no longer pure chance … an exciting adventure. Instead I have the feeling that I have a destiny, in which the events are strung significantly together" (p. 91). Less than two months later she will assert: "I have matured enough to assume my 'destiny,' to cease living an accidental life" (p. 138). What happens in her happens in a scant two-and-a-half years as the restrictive legislation bars "Jews from the paths and the open country [yet] I find life beautiful and I feel free. The sky within me is as wide as the one stretching above my head. I believe in God and I believe in man and I can say so without embarrassment" (p. 151). It is at the end of this period that she begins to formulate expressly theological dicta, in the face of "the latest news … that all Jews will be transported out of Holland … to Poland" (p. 157).

> And yet I don't think life is meaningless. And God is not accountable to us for the senseless harm we cause one another. We are accountable

> to Him! I have already died a thousand deaths in a thousand con-
> centration camps ... And yet I find life beautiful and meaningful.
> From minute to minute. (p. 157)

This capacity for gratitude and praise which she finds within herself moves her in this period of formation beyond humiliation or hate to a newfound peace and freedom: "despite all the suffering and injustice I cannot hate others" (p. 89). "One day I shall surely be able to say to Ilse Blumenthal, 'Do not relieve your feelings through hatred, do not seek to be avenged on all German mothers. ... Give your sorrow all the space and shelter in yourself that is its due ... then you may truly say: "Life is beautiful and so rich ... that it makes you want to believe in God."'" (pp. 100–101).

Yet the God in whom Etty will come to believe is one to whom she introduces us in an entry which takes the form of a prayer:

> Dear God, these are anxious times ... but one thing is becoming
> increasingly clear to me: that you cannot help us, that we must help
> you to help ourselves ... Alas, there doesn't seem to be much You
> Yourself can do about our circumstances, our lives. Neither do I hold
> you responsible. You cannot help us but we must help You and
> defend your dwelling place inside us to the last. (pp. 186–187)

The responsibility she feels is to what has happened within her, and so to the world to which she has come to relate with all that she has. As she writes from Westerbork, in the epilog to the edition of her diaries: "I see more and more that love for all our neighbors ... must take pride of place over love for one's nearest and dearest" (p. 251). The reason is offered in a prayer from her diary which she shares with her friend Tide:

> You have made me so rich, oh God, please let me share out Your
> beauty with open hands. My life has become an uninterrupted dia-
> logue with You, oh God, one great dialogue. (255)

Recording what God is accomplishing in her gives Etty's account its authenticity: not only what she finds herself able to do – in the midst of indescribable misery (p. 245) – but that these capacities come as a continual surprise to herself. Etty Hillesum's spontaneous diaries celebrate the unlocking of "what is truly essential, and deep inside me" (p. 1), and the consequent transformation of a "miserable, frightened creature" (p. 2) into a "soul ... forged out of fire and rock crystal" (p. 241). A soul, moreover, shaped by "an uninterrupted dialogue" which allowed her to make us the gift of her "interrupted life."

What Etty celebrates is a real alteration testifying to a real power at work in the world, granting her a transformed vision: "It still all comes down to the same thing: life is beautiful. And I believe in God – right in the thick of what people call 'horror'" (p. 238). And she addresses these words to her friend Jopie, by way of insisting that such a reality is accessible to her as well. Indeed, what impresses one about Etty's diaries is the precise way in which they articulate a conviction shared by Jew and Christian alike: that life itself, indeed the universe, is a gift. A friend, Klaas, whom she introduces as a "dogged old class fighter" – that is, a confirmed Marxist – was indeed "dismayed and astonished at the same time," and challenged her: "But that – that is nothing but Christianity!" Her response is one we will by now have come to expect: "And I, amused by your confusion, retort quite coolly: 'Yes, Christianity, and why ever not?'" (pp. 222–223). For the historically pockmarked relations between Judaism and Christianity, this response touches a profound nerve, but for present purposes let us simply take it that she has hit upon a shared conviction: that life is a gift. That will suffice to allow us some fruitful reflections on the way in which such convictions function in transforming lives.

Exhibit 4: Jawdat Said – Breezes of Nonviolence in the Hills of the Golan Heights (Afra Jalabi)[8]

Looking at Jawdat Said at his apiary in the rustic village of Birajam in the Golan Heights you would not immediately see his other sides. You would watch him holding and examining the wooden frame within which honey to be collected sits between two thick layers of wax. You would not think this man who is so good at producing honey is also the author of many books and numerous articles and essays. Watching his blue eyes fixated on the frame he just pulled from a box full of hardworking bee you might see his intense focus and dedication coming through but you will not be able instantly to smell the passion he exudes when he discusses the insanity and absurdity of violence in our age or the danger in any thinking that is not comfortable with evolution, or the shame the veto right in the United Nations represents in a modern world claiming democracy and equality. Yet, as the frame is placed in the right metal holders and the honey starts dripping into the barrel, and you begin to talk with him, the ideas start trickling and you will realize you are facing a modern-day Tolstoy. Articulate, passionate, devout yet a rational radical who is deeply feminist.

Jawdat Said is a farmer by day and intellectual by night. He produces tons of healing honey and but more quantities of healing words. Living off the land of his migrating ancestors from the Caucasus, he earns his living from his own manual labor so considers himself a free intellectual. Although he is himself devout and leads an austere and disciplined life which starts before 4 a.m. in the morning, he does not discuss such matters, but rather focuses his discussion on history, philosophy, political theory, and his recent readings. His is a message that would free a person and enable her "second birth," as he calls the breakthrough cultural and traditional barriers.

Even though he is going to turn 80 in 2011, there is something eternally youthful in his face and gestures which always make me see him as the young student in search of the truth, ever present, ever probing and questioning, while rushing around on his bike even to this date. At the age of 11 his mother insisted that he go to al-Azhar to become "educated" like all those who were sent there for its far-reaching reputation.[9] So why would a young student at al-Azhar University be destined to become one of the most articulate modernist voices of an Islamic theory of nonviolence in the Muslim world? There are of course many layers that can eventually

144

find expression in articulate discourse. But more often reformers and creative thinkers are born in a moment of authenticity. And for people working with a rich religious tradition this happens with an echo of eureka while reading Scripture. The young Martin Luther in search of his personal salvation, after great lengths discovered that God's virtue cannot be earned by merit or works but by "faith alone," so turned medieval theology on its head. The young Jawdat Said reading the Qur'an discovered not only that the Qur'an restricts violence but that in most contexts it does not even allow self-defense.

It is not always easy to capture the richness and multilayered thought of Jawdat Said who influenced me in more ways than I am aware of, and who also happens to be my maternal uncle, so both intellectual and personal references intertwine when writing about him, which should also provide an insider view of his journey. Even though he taught me to have a critical mind, especially towards him and his thought, I am aware that I have been most influenced by his historical analytical approach as well as his unique approach to reading the Qur'an. So I wonder if I can even capture in small measure his depth and passion, not to mention his ability to maintain the simplicity and beauty of truth.

When Jawdat was a young teenager sitting in the library in Cairo, lost in his books, a group of his young Syrian friends approached him. They had found a new way to go to heaven without having to do all the rigorous academic work ahead of them which they believed was taking too long to fulfill. They had a shortcut, and they wanted to share their find with their friend. They sat with him and explained that if they went to Palestine and committed to armed Jihad they could spare themselves many years of hard work and would go immediately to heaven as martyrs. Given the eschatological teachings and the doomsday ambiance of al-Azhar and Muslim society in general, Jawdat explains later in an interview, many young students were preoccupied with finding the best ways to be Muslim as well as the easiest way to arrive in heaven. And if the hereafter were so near, maybe academic toil was a waste of time after all. Jawdat listened to them, but he said he needed time to think about their proposal and its premises. He wanted to find out for himself in that moment if the end was really that near, and whether fighting and dying were truly more worthy than studying. His best resource, he decided was the Qur'an, so on that very afternoon, a young scholar was born. Jawdat started rereading the Qur'an, not in the traditional pedagogical way he was being taught, but with burning questions desperately searching for clear answers. He began slowly to realize much of what he was learning not only was not in the Qur'an but was sometimes in dire contrast or opposition to its premises.

One of the issues that started forming in his mind was the issue of jihad. And with this inquisitive attitude he found himself drawn in new directions, during which time he became intimately familiar with the works of Jamaulddin Al-Afaghani, Abdul Rahman Qawakibi, Rashid Rida, and Muhammad Iqbal. Although his young friends' enthusiasm had by then been thwarted, they were still quite exacerbated by Jawdat's many hours at the library and his near lack of social life. And after having become familiar with the discourse of the modernists, Jawdat came upon a small work by the French educated Algerian Malik Bennabi who wrote under the theme of the "Malaise of Civilization," which captivated him as it provided another paradigm shift. Bennabi had coined the phrase "colonizability" to refer to the multiple conditions afflicting Muslims prior to any Western encroachment into their lands. The young Jawdat was fascinated to encounter a discourse whose main focus was not blaming the other, but which used modern analytical frameworks to take a critical look at one's culture and past. His encounters with these inquirers widened the scope of his interest as well as supplying analytical tools beyond those offered at al-Azhar.

In reading Bennabi and Iqbal he was also spurred to reading more history and philosophy and was particularly captured by Arnold Toynbee's historical analysis and his principles of "challenge" and "response" in the rise and fall of civilizations. In addition to new reading habits, he immersed himself in the intellectual and cultural scene of Cairo beyond the confines of al-Azhar. Moreover, he was also witness to political events that deepened his sense of the intellectual and political crisis of Islam, notably the sometimes violent confrontations between the Muslim Brotherhood and the Egyptian government, as well as the assassination of a minister by a militant wing of the Brothers. During this time the Brotherhood was outlawed (1954), with the subsequent imprisonment of over 4000 Brotherhood members, not to mention the assassination of their founder, Hassan al Banna. All this combined with his questioning mind to increase a sense of alarm, deepening his aversion to violence and providing perplexities which demanded further analysis.

After his education in Egypt, Jawdat went to Saudi Arabia to teach, prior to its oil boom, where he lived an austere life among the puritanical Wahhabis, witnessing their simple yet dedicated way of living in small desert towns in Najd. For some time during his youth he had been fascinated by the Wahhabis' call to return directly to the sources, and the ease with which they succeeded in overstepping accumulated tradition, which could have been a natural reaction to the more traditionalist and institutionalized approach of al-Azhar. Yet Jawdat realized the intellectual dangers in so radical an approach, with its static understanding of the cosmos. Wahhabism was ineluctably bound to the past by the way it conceived "following our fathers," a verse of the Qur'an which Jawdat enjoys using to discuss the limitations and sometimes stifling power of a binding tradition. For over the years, his reading of the Qur'an developed in ways that broke him free from the traditionalist atomistic interpretations, often bound to classical medieval works. Such a reading of the Qur'an deepened his dynamic understanding of history and evolution. He found such ideas further validated through Qur'anic notions of "constant creation," with the increase and flow of creation repeated in many verses. Jawdat also traveled to India on a long tour with the Tablighi Jama'a, being drawn to many of their principles and dedication as a way of immersing himself into the different contemporary Muslim expressions.

When Jawdat returned to Syria from Saudi Arabia in 1959, he was drafted into obligatory military service when Syria was allied with Egypt under the title of the United Arab Republic. His principles of disobedience and nonviolence would be put to the test soon after, when several figures in the Syrian army decided to dissolve the Syrian-Egyptian unity through a coup. Jawdat not only protested but spoke out and decided to disobey the orders. He offered to be imprisoned with the senior Egyptian officers who had been already detained. After the situation settled Jawdat was asked to teach ethics in the Syrian Military Academy. When the Ba'thists came to power through a military coup (on March 8, 1963) in the small country still experimenting with democracy in its postcolonial independence, Jawdat resigned and became a professor at a college of education in Damascus. But given the changed political situation, his own political stance assured his "demotion" to various teaching posts, reflecting the hierarchies of power. He was demoted first to a girls' high school, but when he continued to have significant impact there, he was sent to a high school in a rural area 100 km away from Damascus.

The Way of Adam's Son[10]

Jawdat was imprisoned the first time, in early 1965, for his intellectual and political activism, yet after three months was found not guilty of political crimes. Out of prison, with a sense of alarm after witnessing the intellectual and political confusion in the region, he found it urgently necessary to write a book: if not to persuade others, at least to declare his stance publicly. This would be the best way to compose a clear consistent statement of his views and activities, rather than being labeled as one more radical religious intellectual and activist. He published the book in 1966 under the title, *Mathhab Ibn Adam al-Awal: Mushkilat al-U'nf fi al-Amal al-Islami* (*The Way of Adam's First Son: The Problem of Violence in Islamic Activism*). Referring to the son of Adam in the Qur'an who refused to defend himself when his brother decided to kill him, Jawdat wanted to alert emerging Islamic movements to examine seriously and critically the rules and ethics governing resistance and struggle for any kind of reform. Given the challenges of modernity and the issues unresolved in Islamic traditional scholarship and political history, Jawdat urged modern Muslims to become aware that much of what passed as authentic Islamic teaching sometimes deviated sharply from the stringent rules against violence in the Qur'an and in the traditions of the Prophet. Through this and other writings, he tried to articulate ways in which Muslims are bound to uphold what is aligned with truth and justice in any age rather than claim loyalty to a tradition already marked by diverse contexts and historical circumstances. Jawdat did not use words like "nonviolence," nor make any references to Gandhi, Tolstoy, or others, because he wanted to deliver a message to native Muslims that rang true and authentic to their identity and culture, which is why he chose to name this "nonviolent" approach after a radical moment in the Qur'an. "With purpose and insistence I take sentences from the Quran as titles for my books and articles. The discovery of the system of the Quran makes the verses consistent, interconnected without gaps."[11] The "Way of Adam's Son" reflects one of the most clearly nonviolent passages in any scripture, where the first brother refuses to defend himself and accepts instead death. The story in the Qur'an is similar to the biblical passage, but in the Qur'an we find ourselves zooming into the dialog of the two brothers at a critical moment where a humanity pulled by the demand for survival and domination is called to transcend itself into love. In the Qur'an Muhammad is told, "Recite to them the story of Adam's two sons in truth. They each presented a sacrifice. It was accepted from one of them and was not accepted from the other. He said I shall kill you. [That one] said: God accepts from those who are righteous. If you stretch your hand to kill, I shall surely not stretch my hand to kill you. I fear God, the Lord of the Worlds" (Qur'an 5:27–28).

Jawdat finds this elevation of consciousness above the urge to survive to be the pivotal moment,, after which he can show us the way this passage mirrors the intricate moral structure of the rest of the Qur'an. For him, Adam is not an isolated exceptional figure, but the prototype of prophetic figures in the rest of the Qur'an, where all the prophets are shown to be on the Way of Adam's First Son, as each in their different contexts declines self-defense, standing in

149

patience and stillness in the face of harm, committed only to speaking the truth. His book takes us through a list of other encounters in the Qur'an to show the consistency of this model, then offering several Qur'anic examples to show how the prophets witnessed to truth, declining self-defense, so were able to create what he calls "clarity of allegation." He shows how the prophets consistently evidenced a clear intellectual stance: only faith in God. He quotes one Qur'anic verse highlighting how the prophets were rejected not for any harmful or wrong action but simply because they believed. "And they did not deal with them in vengeance for no reason other than that they believed in God, Highest in Glory, Worthy of Praise." (Qur'an 85:8).

Reading the sources directly taught Jawdat that the Qur'an not only proscribes the use of force to spread the word, but even forbids self-defense in most cases, precisely to protect the clarity of the word and the stance it elicits. He finds it intriguing that the Adam's son passage, with a consistent set of parallel passages in the Qur'an, along with the prophet's reference to Adam's son's stance (to be discussed in a moment), escaped a collective triumphalist Muslim imagination as it turned its back on the profound moral implications and practical lessons of the Meccan phase, not to mention two-thirds of the Qur'anic revelation of that period. There is a tendency in Muslim thinking to presume that the later Medina period abrogated the Meccan period, as some Muslims will argue that earlier revelations were abrogated by the sword verse (even though the Qur'an never once used the word "sayf," (sword), in an age saturated with images and poetry about the sword). Moreover, the story of Adam's son belongs to the latest revelations, contradicting claims of abrogation. So Jawdat argues in Ibn Adam that Muslims have to differentiate between founding a movement and holding political authority. Simply put, Jawdat sees the history of Muhammad as one of nonviolent struggle, culminating in a collective movement based on individual consent, which led to treaties with the people of Medina, after which Islam held what can be defined as a city state. And only after having arrived at power with collective consent were Muslims allowed self-defense against the Mecca onslaughts. I also find it telling that Muslims tend to dismiss the nonviolence of the Meccan period, with its clear prohibition of even self-defense, as a situation forced by their small numbers, the same very "weakness" argument generally used to legitimate self-defense and armed struggle. By dismissing the rich and morally consistent nonviolent legacy which established Islam as a religion, a community, and even a city state, Muslims unwittingly reinforce the cheapest allegations against Islam, by which Muhammad is construed as a plotting weakling who laid low until he achieved power. So to remain consistent with its own political devolution into the sword, a community is willing to make a coward of its founder, who was willing with his followers, to die without self-defense in complete surrender to God, following for many years a dedication and commitment rarely matched in history. Jawdat always highlights the ways Muslims tend to use supernatural fantastical interpretations which turn Muhammad's success into a miracle quite beyond history, and human understanding or analysis. Jawdat wants Muslims to examine carefully the way Muhammad aligned himself to truth without coveting political power, and so understand the laws that govern social change based on truth, rather than seek power by any means necessary, which reproduces tyranny into the very systems such groups are aiming to change.

As Jawdat reads early Islamic history, by usurping power through war and force after the fourth elected Muslim caliph, Muslims adapted to the ways of tyranny so could think only of using force to "rectify" things back to the "golden age" of Islam. Such an ideology put the Islamic political system in a perpetual crisis of legitimacy, as each group or dynasty attempted to restore legitimate political authority through illegitimate means. In several of his books and articles, Jawdat shows the way Muslim political thinking failed to understand, let alone articulate, the way prophet Muhammad consolidated collective consent without resorting to violence, as well as the moral and ethical principles governing his nonviolent struggle in Mecca. Furthermore, scholars throughout the ages have failed to see that Medina did not emerge as the result of a military campaign, but was rather the fruit of a committed

151

peaceful movement whose end results not even the prophet himself could have known: a perpetual crisis of political legitimacy which Muslims always sought to remedy through violence. Jawdat carefully delineates the separation of the Word from force, differentiating between persuasion and violent rebellion. As a way of proposing a blueprint of social and political reform through nonviolence, Jawdat carefully discriminates a Jihad legitimate from a Muslim perspective from the Jihad of Khawarij, the first radical religious armed mutiny in early Islamic history. So his book offers a warning to rising Islamic movements about the dangers of militancy and the use of violence in achieving political and social transformation. Long before the rise of militant Islam, he predicted its inevitable crisis. In the recent years some people have been so moved by these accurate predictions of almost half a century that they presumed he was gifted with some spiritual psychic powers. Jawdat laughs heartily at any such suggestion, saying that by careful analysis of a given discourse and enough knowledge of history, one should be able to predict the trajectory of events.

This work of Jawdat marked a profound break from tradition while maintaining at the same time a profound connection to the Qur'an, the conduct of the Prophet and many of his sayings and traditions. Jawdat's commitment to nonviolence represents more than theological conversion or religious idealism. His understanding is couched within a dynamic historical vision in which humanity is evolving and transcending its biological tendencies into aligning to the laws that govern the realm beyond physical and biolevels to an expansion of mercy. Jawdat has been imprisoned five times for his political and religious views. He was tried twice, once by a military court and again by a civil court, yet released by both. When he was imprisoned in 1966, he was transferred to Tadmur's military prison, where he served a year. Once released, he was imprisoned immediately for another year and a half, the longest he endured. He was released in 1969, following a general pardon issued in the aftermath of the 1967 Arab defeat and the loss of the Golan Heights. But as punishment and further isolation due to his views and intellectual activism, he was discharged from teaching or holding any official post. His last imprisonment, in 1973 lasted for nine months.

Although many of his other works do not deal explicitly with violence or nonviolence, he still focuses on the nature of knowledge, power and the implications of coercion with emphasis on the historical laws that govern social and political change. He always urges us to discover an alternative Islamic political theory, in addition to a new theology. Some of his writings have been collected in a six-volume series, entitled *Sunan Taghyir al-Nafs wa l-Mujtama'* (*Laws in the Transformation of Self and Society*). Another of his works, *Hatta Yughayyrir Ma bi-Anfusihim* (*Until They Change What Is Within Themselves*), uses the Qur'anic verse, "That God does not change what is with a people until they change what is within themselves" to explore social change in a framework which examines the dynamics of oppression and injustice.

The death of war

Jawdat always likes to give his audiences a panoramic view of humanity, even a kaleidoscopic image of all the pieces that came together, reminding the listeners of the larger journey our species has come through with the challenges we traversed, then stretching their imagination to the possibilities which could lie ahead. "If within the last ten thousand years we moved out of caves, discovered fire, domesticated animals, created writings and the printing press enabling humanity to condense three-dimensional reality into thin two dimensional paper and preserving knowledge and memory, and how with the invention of electricity even that two dimension is being further condensed into nano technology, where are we going to be ten years from now?" This is how he opens the gates of history to move his audiences and readers beyond the petty ways of our current challenges. Despite what Jawdat sees unfolding around him, he has a deeply optimistic view about humanity's trajectory. "Humanity is still in its infancy" he says in one lecture: "would you give up on a toddler just because he is still not toiled trained or do you see the wonderful adult this little helpless child contains within him?" he asks with a big smile. In another passage Jawdat frequently refers to the story of creation in the Qur'an when discussing the potential of humankind. "When your Lord said to the angels, 'I shall make a Khalipha (viceregent or deputy) on earth.' They said, 'Are you going to place upon it one who will be spreading corruption and spilling blood, while we celebrate your praises and exalt your glory?' He said: 'I know what you know not. And he taught Adam the names of all things.'" (Qur'an 2:30–31). Then in his scrupulous way of picking a phrase Jawdat focuses on God's answer in this passage: the open infinite possibility of a new creation.

Yet Jawdat reminds his audiences or readers in his articles that we are still fulfilling the fears and suspicion of the angels when we engage in violence rather than actualizing God's knowing in us which can respond to the angels' accusations. In an eloquent passage Jawdat turns his historical understanding of war and the use of violence into specific historically limited institutions which may have yielded results in some eras, yet in our age the technology of aggression has rendered aggression itself obsolete. "The nuclear bomb was a stillborn baby. It was born already dead, a tool that cannot be used," he says in his lectures. Jawdat was invited to al-Jazeera in August 2010 for their famous program *al Itijah al-Mu'akiss* (The Opposite Direction) during which he talked about the death of war – an expression which makes many querulous, given the violence endemic to our world, whether they have become inured to the utility of violence or not. During the program he urged Arabs and Muslims to adapt to the reality of our age, in which reason, democracy, and knowledge are the true indices of power which spark movement. For Jawdat, war is already an institution that has run its course. If we really understood its profound implications, 1988 would become a universal anniversary, Jawdat writes, because it was the year humanity started destroying its nuclear weapons. "God's knowledge in his deputy is becoming manifest with the growing consciousness of humanity, and wars have begun to lose their gods and the enthusiasm of their worshippers is thwarting. It is becoming clearer to human beings that war is no longer an inevitable tool to human life, but rather that it is no longer appropriate to human life. This vision did not emerge until this century when the machine of war turned and said so clearly to humanity: If you do not cease to perform this horrific ritual I will destroy you."[12] "What exploded with the dropping of the first nuclear bomb," says Jawdat in many of his lectures, "what exploded was peace" because for him nuclear technology brought us face to face with the dead-end nature of a historically and culturally specific institution that formed during the expansion of extensive agriculture and yet whose end has already happened. We just happen to pay tribute and respect to an outdated deity whose rituals and "horrific rites" capture our out-dated collective imagination when reality is showing clearly that it no longer an option. So for Jawdat the wars that exist today are the remaining pockets of an obsolete institution in an era where equal powers can no longer engage in warfare.

In 2000 Dr Azizah al-Hibri commissioned a paper for a special issue on Islam of the *Journal of Law and Religion*, "Law, Religion, and the Prophetic Method of Social Change." And in 2003, the *Journal of Law and Religion* at Hamline University awarded him its Lifetime Achievement Award for creative scholarship and many years of intellectual activism. In 2009 Jawdat was invited to the European Union, to a symposium on the Role of Religious Actors in Areas of Conflict, organized by the Bishops' Conferences of the European Union (COMECE) where he stated his position:

> You are now discussing the role of the religious actors in areas of conflict. But I would like to say that all of earth is an area of conflict, and the smaller local conflicts and regional wars are only a reflection of the greater corruption that afflicts the United Nations. The privilege the Great Powers want to preserve as a monopoly is the seed of all evils. As long as justice is not presented as the viable choice in resolving these conflicts, as long as we all revere and worship force and as long as we sit mute and in complacency before the veto right in the Security Council which is hindering the onward march of humanity; as long as we maintain these conditions there will neither be peace nor security in this world. We read in the Quran, "nor did we destroy the cities unless its people were unjust." (Qur'an 28:59).

There, Jawdat also presented his view of the European Union as a new political threshold in human history:

> the European Union has ushered the era of the Word of Equality. I consider it a human threshold and one of humanity's greatest achievements. The European Union stands today as the crown of the human mind. These nations came to embrace and believe in that which is most sacred in religions; they agreed not to take one another for gods, at least among themselves. They liberated themselves from Napoleon and Hitler, and of the culture that made both. This was not a gift from heaven, but grew from pain and suffering and the payment of a heavy price. Napoleon and Hitler could both unite Europe, but only by force and coercion. Today they are united by the human mind, this creature of God which understood lessons of history after trying war of all possible variety; the One-hundred Years War, the Thirty Years War, religious wars, sectarian wars and world wars which exacted hundreds of millions of human sacrifices. This union is not expanding by military conquest or annexation, but by the consent of the parties involved, with a statement of benefits and gains; no one loses and everyone wins. It is a voluntary expansion. Countries are pleading to join, saying accept us and we will abide by your terms. This is an obvious conquest. True that you [the European Union] have not united the world, but you have created the foundations up on which the world can unite. This is nearer to the religion of God, and to His Messengers, and the true nature of humankind than of all people have tried throughout history. It is a new event in history.

Since the Dalai Lama also sees the EU as a promising new development in history perhaps it was not a coincidence that the two men met at Castelgandolfo in Rome at the Third Synthesis Dialogues organized by the Association of Global New Thought. Jawdat and the Dalai Lama enjoyed each other's similar phrases about "having come out of the muscle age into the age of the nervous system."

Despite his love for a frugal and simple life he is openly enthusiastic about today's communications technologies, with a thrill nearly identical to today's youth, equipping the mosque in the village with a computer and a video camera. He is always thrilled to follow the new innovations to follow the ways they are democratizing our

156

world and facilitating the spread of information and knowledge. My cousins helped him to learn the computer and navigate the Internet, and with my help he learned touch-typing more than ten years ago. Yet despite this comfort and positive outlook on technology he never lost his awe of and love for nature. With him I am reminded that we live truly in fantastic times: that we are a generation that can live frugally, simply while also being able to reach the end of the earth in the blink of an eye, or even download an entire book from a distant bookstore to read on a magical plate.

Many in the Arab World, and the world over, will introduce Jawdat as the Arab Gandhi, which I see fitting, given his radical nonviolence, thin figure and utter frugality, yet I sometimes call him the Circassian Tolstoy because of his connection to the land, nature and his passionate connection to Scripture. And there are times when I feel I am sitting with a completely free Buddha who discovered a path that is not so clear or open to the rest of us with such mental clarity, an irrevocable trust in God, and a lifestyle to match. But he is also uniquely Jawdat Said, completely his own person. What impacts me personally and I find truly inspiring is his deeply private devotion and personal ethics bordering on the severe, yet in the simplicity of a lifestyle a person who is publicly radical and forward looking on political, scientific, and social issues of our planet. The deliciousness of the honey he produces at his apiary can only be matched by the wonderful taste of freedom he inspires in those around him. Spending time with him I am always reminded of the sweetness of honesty, the dignity of manual labor and how rich we already are under starry nights and the fragrance of jasmine trees and the open and tremendous heritage of humanity available to us now, and how fantastically empowered we already are when we decide to believe, only believe.

What Can These Lives Tell Us?

If one focuses on "the experience itself" – whatever that might be – of transformation, then the accounts may be contingently related to what it is that we cannot help but remark in the person before us. But when we are privileged enough to have access to the narrative account, we come to appreciate how these narratives are shaped by sets of convictions which can otherwise be expressed as doctrines of specific religious traditions, where the fact that doctrines shape narratives reminds us that they do not play a theoretical but a *grammatical* role in the lives of the faithful.[13] They do not, in short, offer to explain a reality behind the One to whom individuals like Etty respond, but rather provide the manner in which their respective responses offer us access to the reality revealed in their transformations. Doctrine, in other words, both comes to life and is embodied in the response of those whom we cannot but recognize to be saints. It is obvious enough how doctrine "comes to life" there, but how can we say that it is *embodied* in such lives? The argument here is at once simple and subtle: it turns on the fact that we will always be forced to speak of religious matters in a language which is inherently analogous. The term "transformation" offers a handy example. Any formula we give for it will contain terms of a like quality – terms whose "open texture" or "systematic ambiguity" will demand that we offer an example to establish our "frame of reference" or "benchmark" usage.[14] And it is precisely individuals who provide the living examples to anchor our usage – a commonplace yet remarkable situation which accounts for the fact that we can recognize such exemplary individuals without always being able to *say* what it is that makes them such. Yet their narrative accounts, when available, can be found to be structured in such a way as to be shaped by what we otherwise call doctrinal statements. That is the way in which their lives embody doctrine.[15]

What, then, are we to do with the further fact that distinct lives may embody diverse doctrines, and yet each exhibit a comparable transformation? (We may even presume that their respective accounts can be shown to embody different doctrinal positions.) Celebrate it, I contend, for so far we have no way of placing ourselves in the position of comparing or ranking religious traditions. I am not pontificating, insisting that we cannot do so; in fact, I suspect that we must. I am only remarking that we are not *yet* in a position to do so. We must acquire a set of intellectual skills allowing us to compare cultural frameworks. In fact, nothing so effectively displays the cultural particularity of Christianity as the emergence of a postcolonial world, in which Western Christians found themselves facing other religious traditions yet were no longer able to presume an accustomed superiority. Yet how are we to respond conceptually to such novelty? By reminding ourselves, I would suggest, that responses are structured by traditions whose doctrinal patterns provide the grammar of the response. Insofar as those doctrinal patterns shape and give direction to a lived response in such a way that it issues in an authentic transformation, then we must acknowledge them to be true, much as the aim and correlative skills of an archer allow his arrow to find its mark. This strategy keeps us from directly comparing statements lifted out of different traditions, and reminds us that such statements – if they be religious statements – subserve that transforming relationship which we have noted through Etty's narrative. Yet *within* each functioning tradition, there will be a set of shaping beliefs or doctrines, the truth of which will (or will not) be exhibited in the life of the community, especially in its notable exemplars. And where those exemplary individuals tell their story, as Etty has, astute critics will be able to discern the doctrinal patterns which give their narratives a structure distinctive to the community in which they partake. Such is the grammar of the matter: lives are rendered in narratives which display a structure; we are compelled by the lives, inspired and illuminated by the narratives, and guided by what we can discover of their structure.

What have we given up, in trying to respond to the new situation of religious and cultural diversity? *Not* the "truth claims" of particular religious traditions, but rather a presumptive way of ranking them. *Not* the certitude which Newman attributes to faith, whereby we freely give "real assent" to what is offered us as liberating and life-giving, but a monocultural attitude of *certainty* in which we know that we are right.[16] What we have recovered is an attitude of critical modesty towards our modes of expression, which could help us recover a similar modesty displayed by medieval thinkers, and use it to profit from a situation which appears so unsettling.

159

We have long overlooked just how intercultural and interreligious the medieval world really was.[17] Take, for example, Aquinas's account of religious language, in which he used a sophisticated semantics to clarify and extend Moses Maimonides' views on attributing perfections to divinity. The portion of that account pertinent here is Aquinas's insistence that phrases like "God is just" can be said properly but imperfectly of divinity.[18] By exploring how expressions might "imperfectly signify" divinity, we can be led to see how one tradition may complement another, and so use the encounter with alternative conceptualities to enrich our own. That is, I believe, the sense of Etty's cool retort: "Yes, Christianity, and why ever not?" Far from a call to syncretism, that response appreciates a power peculiar to the Gospels by appropriating them to her situation. These complementarities work quite well in practice, as the faithful in distinct traditions find themselves drawn to incorporate prayer patterns from one another, much as Jung remarked (in 1948) in reference to a division within Western European Christianity: that every cultured European he knew was either a Catholic Protestant or a Protestant Catholic.[19]

But what of that further assessment, to which we seem inevitably drawn, which would compare traditions by ranking them? I have already noted that we are not yet in a position to do that, and I emphasize the "yet" not because I believe we may one day be able to, but to remind us how unskilled we are in comparing across cultural and conceptual frameworks. The immediate alternative of accepting the picture of religious traditions as several ways up one mountain is attractive but it begs the central question by incorporating an answer. It offers a useful antidote, of course, to the need for pre-emptive certainty, as does our strategy of locating doctrines as the grammar structuring accounts of personal transformation. I find Wilfrid Cantwell Smith's programmatic suggestions in his *Towards a World Theology* helpful by pointing to ways in which we could develop the skills required for fruitful comparative study: a seminar composed of articulate believers from distinct traditions, in which communication would be deemed to be achieved when each person could understand the other's account as one in which they could plausibly participate.[20] Exercises of this sort, carried out regarding specific doctrines-cum-practices, might well be able to help those participating develop skills of comparative assessment. We might discover, for example, that the "distinction" of God from the world is more ably secured in a tradition which was also forced to articulate how two natures functioned in one person (Christ) than in the other two faiths which avow creation, even though there are powerfully analogous connections between all three in this regard.[21] In virtue of live encounters, however, we in the West are becoming more and more aware of the threshold on which we stand, which allows us to inquire into our own traditions (in the spirit of "faith seeking understanding") as they now face other major religious traditions with palpable histories of holiness.

Indeed, this "convergence-in-difference" which characterizes interfaith exchange today, and is so abundantly exemplified in the lived narrative of Etty Hillesum, offers a fresh appreciation of a "conversion" from the social imaginaries of our "secular age" to which Charles Taylor's rigorously convoluted journey carries us. Our exploration is much indebted to his historical and analytic skills, especially as they incisively delineate our "secular age," indeed celebrating the openings this "age" has extended to us all, only to suggest how exemplary individuals have discovered ways beyond its confining parameters. At the same time, I have attempted to make more explicit what his analysis does note and presume, by identifying what may move those individuals to find the parameters of the age confining, and so to seek for ways beyond them: that "wonderment" which embodies our sense of the radical contingency of the universe, prompting us to connect what we see and feel with "something more." Moreover, the plethora of ways in which that connection may be intimated hardly weakens but rather enhances our need to discover it.

Notes

1   Michael Prior, *Bible and Colonialism* (Sheffield: Sheffield Academic Press, 1997).

2 Charles Taylor, *A Secular Age* (Cambridge, MA: Belknap Press of Harvard University Press, 2007).

3 Rabia Terri Harris, "Nonviolence in Islam: The Alternative Community Tradition," in Daniel L. Smith-Christopher (ed.), *Subverting Hatred: The Challenge of Nonviolence in Religious Traditions* (Maryknoll, NY: Orbis Books, 1998), pp. 95–114, at p. 101. See the four-volume study of Louis Massignon, *The Passion of al-Hallaj, Mystic and Martyr of Islam* (trans. Herbert Mason; Princeton, NJ: Princeton University Press, 1975), and Herbert Mason's dramatic précis, *The Death of al-Hallaj* (Notre Dame, IN: University of Notre Dame Press, 1979).

4 Mary Louise Gude, CSC, *Louis Massignon: The Crucible of Compassion* (Notre Dame, IN: University of Notre Dame Press, 1996).

5 William Dalrymple, "A New Deal in Pakistan," *New York Review of Books* 55:5 (April 3, 2008) at p. 16.

6 This section is adapted from my *Faith and Freedom* (Oxford: Blackwell, 2004), ch. 16, pp. 249–252.

7 *An Interrupted Life* (New York: Simon & Schuster, 1985) and more recently, *Letters from Westerbork* (New York: Pantheon, 1987), now combined in a single edition (New York: Henry Holt, 1996), from which page references here will be taken.

8 This section is written by Afra Jalabi. Afra Jalabi has been a columnist for the past 10 years (for the London-based *Al Jadeedah* magazine and the Saudi-based *al-Yaum* newspaper), and is a member of the editorial board of the *Journal of Law and Religion*. Her interests lie in the theory of nonviolence, early Islamic history and texts, feminist theory, and Qur'anic exegesis. She has lectured about these themes in Canada and the United States, and is currently a PhD candidate at Concordia University in Montreal.

9 Jawdat shares personal reflections about his youth in an interview in the Iranian magazine, *Majllat Qadya Islamiyah Mu'assirah*, available on his website, www.jawdatsaid.net, which has his books, articles in addition to some translated pieces into English and French.

10 *Madhab Ibn Adam al-Awal: Mushkilat al-Unf fi l-Amal al-Islami* (*The Way of Adam's First Son: The Problem of Violence in Muslim Activism*) (1st edn, Damascus 1966; 5th edn, Beirut: Dar al-Fikr al-Mu'asir, 1993).

11 Column in *Al-Majalah* Magazine (no. 1109) May 13–19, 2001.

12 *Madhab Ibn Adam*, p. 60.

13 A synoptic exploration of this sense of doctrine has been fruitfully carried out by George Lindbeck in his *Nature of Doctrine* (Philadelphia, PA: Westminster, 1985).

14 See James Ross, *Portraying Analogy* (Cambridge: Cambridge University Press, 1982), and for the history of these matters, my *Analogy and Philosophical Language* (New Haven: Yale University Press, 1973).

15 See Robert Barron, *And Now I See* (New York: Continuum, 1998).

16 John Henry Newman, *An Essay in Aid of a Grammar of Assent* (Notre Dame, IN: University of Notre Dame Press, 1979), with perceptive introduction by Nicholas Lash.

17 See my *Knowing the Unknowable God: Ibn-Sina, Maimonides, and Aquinas* (Notre Dame, IN: University of Notre Dame Press, 1986).

18 See Herbert McCabe's appendix, "Signifying Imperfectly," in *Summa Theologiae* 1.12–13 (*Knowing and Naming God*) (New York: McGraw-Hill, 1964).

19 C.G. Jung, *Psychology of the Transference* (Princeton, NJ: Princeton University Press, 1966), p. 30.

20 Wilfred Cantwell Smith, *Towards a World Theology* (Philadelphia, PA: Westminster Press, 1981), pp. 98–101.

21 See my "The Christian Distinction Celebrated and Expanded," in John Drummond and James Hart (eds), *The Truthful and the Good* (Dordrecht: Kluwer, 1996), for an attempt to extend Robert Sokolowski's "Christian distinction" in his *God of Faith and Reason* (note 8) to all Abrahamic faiths.

7

Respectfully Negotiating Outstanding Neuralgic Issues: Contradictions and Conversions

We have so far treated differences among these Abrahamic traditions on a par with similarities; indeed, often folded difference into a larger common scheme. While this has served the primary intention of this inquiry, it may also have appeared to be too irenic. What about the classic neuralgic issues which preoccupied medieval disputations, many of which continue to emerge as front-line challenges in casual conversation between Jews and Christians, or between Muslims and Christians? Obvious candidates would be vastly different interpretations of Scripture, "trinity," "incarnation," and "original sin" as Christian doctrines; Muslim attitudes towards the central icon of Christian, the "crucified one," as well as sheer Christian incomprehension in the face of claims to a fresh revelation in Arabia in the seventh century after Christ. The adage that dialog is between persons rather than doctrines suggests an initial approach to softening the abrasive impact of doctrinal standoff, as in the claim that Christians believe, while Muslims deny, that God has a son! For in conversation, persons can offer the sort of qualifications

Towards a Jewish-Christian-Muslim Theology, First Edition. David B. Burrell.
© 2011 John Wiley & Sons Ltd. Published 2011 by John Wiley & Sons Ltd.

which would attenuate suspicion of contradiction in that exchange about "God having a son" or not. Differences will indeed remain, but of a sort which can lead each interlocutor to a clearer statement of what they believe, and may even foster mutual understanding. So let us adopt this approach by simulating probing conversations as we explore these neuralgic issues in order: (1) diverse ways of interpreting a scripture ostensibly held in common (Jews and Christians); (2) barely compatible understandings of scripture itself as the "Word of God" (Christians and Muslims); (3) Christian doctrinal positions antithetical both to Jews and to Muslims – "trinity," "incarnation," and "original sin"; (4) Muslim "attitudes towards the crucified one"; and finally (5) the stubborn fact that Christians find claims to a fresh revelation in Arabia in the seventh century after Christ virtually oxymoronic. A daunting agenda, certainly, yet as we set ourselves to unravel longstanding knots in each case, the preliminary ground-breaking of previous chapters can supply us with a set of strategies to bring to bear on that task.

Diverse Ways of Interpreting a Scripture Ostensibly Held in Common (Jews and Christians)

We noted at the outset how the chronological relations that obtain between different Abrahamic faiths leads quite naturally to later ones presuming to supersede the earlier. Nowhere is this more in evidence than the way Christians will (to a Jewish mindset) pillage the Hebrew Scriptures for evidence presaging the mission of Jesus. Yet treating the Hebrew Scriptures as a palimpsest limning the face of Jesus need not have been offensive in itself, until Paul made clear that Jesus' saving mission to all nations could be executed quite independently of the carefully crafted pastiche of *mitzvot* that suffused Jewish life. The key New Testament text is Acts 15:7–11, ever celebrated in Christian history as a liberation:

> As the discussion [whether to circumcise non-Jews as part of their initiation into the new community] became heated, Peter stood up

and said to them: "Brothers, you know what God did among us in the early days, so that non-Jews could hear the good news from me and believe. God, who can read hearts, put himself on their side by giving the Holy Spirit to them just as he did to us. He made no distinction between us and them and cleansed their hearts through faith. So why do you want to put God to the test? Why do you lay on the disciples a burden which neither our ancestors or we were able to carry? We believe, indeed, that we are saved through the grace of the Lord Jesus, just as they are."

As a consequence of decisions like this, Jewish interpretive strategies were further elaborated to the point where the two communities, in practice, could hardly claim to agree on the way that Hebrew Scripture addressed human actions; that is, purported to be a divine revelation guiding the life and learning of a community. The trenchant statement in this regard of John of the Cross – hardly a polemicist – is telling:

When he gave us, as he did, his Son, who is his one Word, he spoke everything to us, once and for all in that one Word. There is nothing further for him to say. This is the meaning of the passage that St. Paul begins with when he tried to persuade the Hebrews to abandon the primitive ways and means of treating with God, which are in the Law of Moses, and fix their eyes on Christ alone.[1]

Put starkly, Christians have transformed what remains the setting for Jews' daily life into stage-setting for the advent of God's definitive revelation in His own Son, the very Word by which God creates the universe. While God remains professedly the same, the ways of seeking and finding God have been radically reconfigured as this community intent on following Jesus comes to discover and propose ways in which Jesus brings those same Scriptures to an unprecedented focus. Paul's letter to the Philippians (1:8–11) offers a hint of what will replace the traditional *mitzvot*, remembering that these same Philippians had never tasted life guided by the Torah:

God knows that I love you dearly with the love of Christ Jesus, and in my prayers I ask that your love may lead you each day to a deeper knowledge and clearer discernment, that you may have good criteria

167

for everything. So you may be pure of heart and come blameless to the day of Christ, filled with the fruit of holiness which comes through Christ Jesus, for the glory and praise of God.

And as the movement gained ground quite in ignorance of the ground which originally nourished God's revelation in Jesus, Jewish efforts to recapitulate their community approached the Torah with an inherently defensive and increasingly sclerotic attitude, in the face of this internal challenge as well as in the wake of the devastating Roman destruction of the center of their liturgical life in Jerusalem. So the "rabbinic Judaism" which resulted only served to confirm a growing conviction among followers of Jesus – Jewish and Gentile alike – that vitality lay with them, as the original covenant had become "old" in the face of the "new," even if the way the new Judaism emerged, in reacting to the new movement, would make it the younger of the two.

Yet as the labels "old" and "new" settled into place, and with the "new Israel" incorporating itself into imperial Rome, Jews became the "other" in the midst of an enveloping "Christendom," implicitly confirming that "new" replaced "old," so gradually denying in practice the heritage and promise distinctive to Jews. So that faith in Jesus, which Paul had hoped would knit Jew and Gentile together, came rather to display an implacable hatred for God's original people as those who had rejected (and inexplicably continued to reject) the offer made to them by their God's only Son. So two separate worlds developed, one politically dominating and encompassing the other while claiming theological superiority, with each preferring to have nothing to do with the other. As Ignaz Maybaum puts it:

> Two thousand years of Christianity have been two thousand years of hatred for the Jews. This is certainly no exaggeration. Rosensweig even speaks of eternal hatred for the Jew. If the Second Vatican Council really means a change in this respect, it would be an apocalyptic event, bringing blessing not only to the Jews but to the whole of mankind. ...[2]

A Reform rabbi who found refuge in England in the 1930s, Maybaum is not an inciter but a sober analyst; he is simply telling it like Jews see and feel it. (Since he realized early on the necessity of bringing Jews, Christians, and Muslims together, we shall invoke his prescient vision more than once in what follows.)

We must acknowledge that "hatred" is the appropriate word, finding expression in disdain that could easily find expression in outright persecution, and from upstanding Christians who were outraged to find Jews unable to read their Scriptures as presaging the coming of Jesus. The result of such longstanding disdain was evident in the virtual paralysis of Germany's Christian population in the face of the systematic public genocide meted out by a neo-pagan Nazi regime to its Jewish citizens. As Ignaz Maybaum insists, the very ability to desensitize a population to such horrors cannot even be approached in other than theological terms:

> The Jew hatred which Hitler inherited from the medieval church made Auschwitz the twentieth-century Calvary of the Jewish people. (p. 158).

But it also spelt the death of a blithe humanism:

> Only the biblical view of the world as the creation of God and every human being as created in the image of God can save us from the catastrophe looming on the horizon of a civilization alienated from God the creator of heaven and earth. (p. 159)

That theme, enunciated here in 1965 (the year *Nostra Aetate* was promulgated) has recently been reiterated in the *Common Word between Us*, issued by more than 200 Muslim intellectual leaders in the wake of Pope Benedict XVI's Regensburg address, offering the leitmotif of this extended inquiry.[3] For *Nostra Aetate* had celebrated the fact that Muslims, as well as Jews and Christians, avow the free creation of the universe by one God, which some have already mined to discover the way medieval exchanges explored that avowal, and which *A Common Word* has more recently tracked in the hope of world peace.

It is hardly surprising that followers of Jesus would proceed to delineate ways in which God's revelation in Jesus brought the

Hebrew Scriptures to an unprecedented focus, leading to fresh readings of those same Scriptures. Yet 19 centuries later (in *Nostra Aetate)*, by privileging Paul's insistence that "God does not take back his gifts nor renege on his promises" (Rom. 11:29), those same followers would repudiate the hatred germinated by widespread church disdain of those committed to the original covenant. It is in that spirit that Ignaz Maybaum can show his fellow Jews that "the doctrine of the Trinity, rejecting various forms of Gnostic heresy, ensured that Christians, like Jews, glorified God as benevolent creator," "prevent[ing] a theology which would have bypassed the creator God of the Jews and worshipped the Logos instead" (pp. 71, 72). When we explore this doctrine-in-the-making, we shall identify the operative constant of the "gigantic mental struggle" to formulate this doctrine as the *shema*: "hear O Israel, God our God is One" (Deut. 6:4). Maybaum's observations capture the spirit of this inquiry, as we attempt to uncover questions to which the formulations proper to each tradition intend to respond. In that way, by locating similar queries at work in each tradition, we find ourselves able to trace formulations which appear to contradict, or to affront the other, to the matrix from which they have emerged, and so render them intelligible in terms proper to them, as Maybaum has done with Christian efforts to formulate one God as "Father, Son, and Holy Spirit." The strategy we owe to Bernard Lonergan, who never failed to remind his students that we could never understand the formulations crafted in early Christian centuries as answers unless we attended to the questions to which they responded. A similar hermeneutic must attend comparative theological inquiry, as we shall see in exploring specific theological topics.

Barely Compatible Understandings of Scripture itself as the "Word of God" (Christians and Muslims)

If Jews and Christians, who regularly pray the same Psalms, can still diverge starkly when interpreting the Scripture they ostensibly hold in common, divergences between Christians and Muslims are yet more radical. For while Bible and Qur'an are each regarded by their respective communities as the Word of God, so treated as "holy books," those very communities consider them very differently. While it is virtually impossible to find a single Jewish view on the Hebrew Scriptures (*TaNaK*), Jews and Christians can be said to subscribe to some form of "inspiration," however that may be understood. Indeed, the notion is best left vague enough to ascribe some trace of "divine influence" without specifying it any further. This allows, of course, members of the community (aligned or not with the *ethos* of each respective community) to range from "inspirational" to inerrant text, from poetry to the "literal word of God." So along a spectrum, communities and individuals will variously countenance diverse forms of "source criticism," yet none will dispute that the manner of composition of the text, together with the identity of its authors (where available) is relevant to understanding its meaning. Indeed, the vague term "inspiration" intends to leave room for this.

Authorial sources for the Qur'an, however, are deemed irrelevant, if not oxymoronic. Moreover, if the Qur'an can be said to be a book, it is rather "the book" (*al-qur'an*). Here the very term must be parsed analogously, to be faithful to its different uses in each Abrahamic faith. That is why the ostensibly inclusive Arabic expression, "people of the book" (*ahl al-kitab*), rather functions politically than theologically. Now we might begin to grasp why it is simply inappropriate for others to demand that Muslims acknowledge "source criticism" with regard to the Qur'an. Indeed, contemporary Jews or Christians tend to consider any unwillingness here to be a cardinal sign that Muslims "have not undergone the enlightenment," with the implication that their view of the Qur'an means that every Muslim is *ipso facto* a "fundamentalist." An apposite comparison with Orthodox Judaism should help here, where scriptural interpretation is always subject to an extensive commentary tradition. Qur'an commentaries tend to appear regularly in each epoch; so only those who forego such assistance to turn directly to the Qur'an itself, merit the title "fundamentalist," and their orientation can usually be traced to Western biblical attitudes rather than to their own tradition.

A better way to detect the attitudes each tradition takes towards its Scriptures is to observe how these Scriptures are utilized in life and worship, rather than inquire what some adherents might *think* about their status – as "God's Word" or whatever. Here it is fair to say that the Qur'an supplies Muslims who regularly invoke it with the air they breathe, regularly substituting that pure air for a sur- rounding environment that could be polluted. Indeed, the Qur'an heard or recited fashions the times of prayer which punctuate each day. Once we appreciate this fact, we will be less preoccupied whether those reciting it can understand it in their own language. The Christian analog here is choral or chanted worship rather than a didactic sermon, so some Christians will be more able to resonate with an Arabic Qur'an than others. Anyone familiar with the public call to prayer in Islamic societies will appreciate this rhythm. And that appreciation could well prepare them to hear how the Qur'an as Word of God is closer to Jesus (who is Word of God for Muslims as well as Christians) than to the Bible. Here the parallel formulas evidence similarity-cum-difference:

> Qur'an is the Word of God made Arabic [book]
> Jesus is the Word of God made human.

The operative similarity even suggests that the Qur'an is more than a book, as indeed it is for Muslims, who regularly invoke names of God, from a canonical list of 99 culled from the Qur'an, in a given order, assisted by a *subha* of 33 prayer beads.[4]

So the difference between Bible and Qur'an would appear to be more than one of degree: that Muslims venerate their book more than Christians do theirs, though each will call their book "holy." The difference verges on the "ontological": the Qur'an presents God's very Word, so the names found there are names by which God names God's own self, granting them iconic status suffused with divine power for those who recite them attentively. (Annemarie Schimmel speaks, as we shall see, of "inlibration".) The best analogy one can make with Christianity is receiving the body of the Lord in communion. Cabbalist Judaism offers analogous methods of interiorizing the text of Scripture by releasing the divine power latent in the words of Scripture, even if Jewish tradition forbears vesting Hebrew Scripture itself with the same divine power Muslims find in the Qur'an. Another way to mark the difference between these two (or perhaps three) "books" is to note the practices in which each community engages so as to "read" them properly. While all communities use their Scriptures in prayer, denoting a signal place where Jews and Christians converge, in praying the Psalms; Jews can be found *studying* Torah, while Christians have access to a meditative mode called *lectio divina*, and Muslims normally experience the Qur'an *recited*; so we have *study*, *lectio*, and *recitation*, all three of which Paul Griffiths analyzes in his *On Reading*.[5] We shall further comment on the differences for more specifically doctrinal contexts.

Christian Doctrinal Positions Antithetical both to Jews and to Muslims: "Trinity," "Incarnation," "Original Sin"

We have already noted Ignaz Maybaum's generous reading of the Christian doctrine of "trinity," and Annemarie Schimmel's use of the neologism "inlibration" to gesture towards Islamic parallels to "incarnation." So let us consider each of these historically neuralgic points in order, beginning with that of "trinity," to illustrate how interfaith exchange can now offer an apt vehicle for developing doctrine. Christian–Muslim disputations regularly opposed Muslim insistence on the unicity of God to a Christian trinitarian presentation. Yet every student of the history of Christian thought knows that it took four to five centuries of christological controversies, plus another century of conceptual elaboration, to hone a "doctrine of trinity," precisely because of the *shema*: "Hear, O Israel, God our God is one" (Deut. 6:6). If Muslim teaching showcasing divine unity – *tawhid* – has been developed polemically over against a misunderstanding of the "threeness" of the one God, that should be perfectly understandable for Christians, given the time it took them to articulate "threeness" in God without prejudice to God's unity. Moreover, Islamic thought soon came to see how, as God's Word, the Qur'an must be co-eternal with God, lest God be mute![6] So once we emphasize the Johannine expression of "word," rather than the synoptic usage of "son," in dialog with Muslims, we will at once be able to converse with them less polemically, yet also realize how thoroughly our baptismal formula refines the ordinary notion of *son*. And rather than diminishing the presentation of our faith, we will have come to a more refined understanding of what we have long been affirming. The fact remains that our faith is indeed "trinitarian" while theirs is not, yet the process of dialog will have brought us to a better articulation of our respective understandings of *trinity* and of *unity* in God.

The next example comes as a corollary to the intra-divine relations, called (in common parlance) "persons" yet utterly different from the distinct individuals we normally identify as persons. We are speaking of the mediating role of Jesus in effecting our relationship to God. Muslims insist that while the Prophet delivers the Qur'an, which presents us with the very Word of God, it is our response to God's very Word which effects an immediate relation with God. Given the gift of the Qur'an, there can be no need for a "mediator," nor should one think of Muhammad as one. On the other hand, Christian Scripture and theology speaks in countless ways of Jesus Christ as "mediator between God and human beings." Now the ordinary use of "between" makes it sound as though Jesus operates in a space between the creator and creatures. Yet that would be an Arian view, explicitly repudiated in the early councils, so in orthodox Christian belief Jesus' mediation operates theandrically; that is, as something intrinsic to Jesus' divine-human constitution, carefully elaborated in early councils from Nicaea to Chalcedon. So while the actions of Jesus can effect an immediate relation to God as Father, Jesus does not mediate as a "go-between."

So the very feature of mediation which Muslims deny to the Prophet, thinking that to be Jesus' manner of mediating, represents

174

a distortion of Christian thought, though one in fact proposed by some Christians as well. One thinks of sixteenth-century debates between Protestants and Catholics, where the polemical edge doubtless distorted a more classical meaning of "mediation." For Catholics have elaborated a sense of "mediator" to include ecclesial structures and personages, so that ordained persons "mediate" the saving power of God to the faithful. But just as Jesus could not be construed, thanks to the *shema*, as a "being alongside God" (which is the meaning Muslims attach to *shirk*: something – either created or uncreated – on a par with the creator), so Christians falsify their own faith if they conceive of Jesus' mediation (or, *a fortiori*, that of the church) as situated "between" the creator and creatures. As the Word who is God, Jesus' mediation effects that immediate relation to God as Father which Christians presume in their recurrent prayer: "Our Father."

The final example explores the polemical stance both Jews and Muslims take with regard to Christian teaching regarding "original sin." Here again, applying Aquinas's hermeneutical caution, to clarify the propositions of faith as well as scrutinize arguments employed, we find that there are widely divergent versions of "original sin" in diverse Christian lexicons, and one is never sure which one of them is at issue. The spectrum of meanings Christians attach to this teaching can be fairly represented between a characteristically Catholic view, captured in Chesterton's insistence that "original sin is the only empirically verified Christian doctrine" (or "Murphy's Law" in the moral order), to the stark contention that its effects render our intellectual and voluntary faculties utterly dysfunctional. But these views require that Adam's transgression somehow affect and infect us all by a path which remains obscure, as Rudi te Velde's delineation of Aquinas's attempt shows so clearly.[7] So they all focus on the universal human need for redemption, exemplified in and effected by Jesus' death on a cross. Now if this remains a sticking point for Muslims, an adequate way of articulating "the atonement" continues to elude Christian theology, which deems Anselm's account deficient on several counts, but has yet to find a satisfactory formulation (though I find one in Sebastian Moore's *The Crucified Jesus Is No Stranger*[8]).

Yet we all recognize rational creatures to be incapable of achieving unaided their inbuilt goal of union with God, so some action on the creator's part must make that possible. Now a closer look at the Muslim view of human beings' capacity for "drawing near to" God shows less difference between us than first appeared. Islamic thought takes the situation in the Hejaz before the Prophet's preaching the Qur'an, and readily applies it to the entire world: bereft of divine revelation, human beings are bound to wonder aimlessly, seeking to fulfill their own desires and inevitably engaging in deadly combat. (This we see every day, of course, as we all experience Paul's rendition of "original sin": "I do not do what I want, but on the contrary, the very things I hate" (Rom. 7:15).) On this view, the Torah or the "Injil" (gospel, i.e. New Testament) serves the purpose for Jews or Christians that the Qur'an does for Muslims, since human beings left to themselves would never make it. So while Christianity focuses on the death and resurrection of Jesus, Muslims locate the redemptive act *par excellence* in the unmerited and serendipitous "coming down" of the Qur'an from God through the Prophet.[9] Human beings are invited to respond to this gift, with their everlasting redemption turning on the quality of that response. This dynamic reinforces the fundamental analogy between Jesus and the Qur'an: as Christians believe Jesus to be the Word of God made human, Muslims believe the Qur'an to be the word of God made book. So each of these examples can show us how comparative inquiry will inevitably highlight dimensions of our own theological task, by accentuating items in our own traditions which need clarification and development.

Muslim Attitudes towards the Crucified

As Paul himself discerned, a crucified Messiah can only be a scandal to Jews and nonsense to non-Jews (1 Cor. 1:23). So it is hardly surprising that Muslims take umbrage at Jesus crucified or that Jews find it bizarre; indeed, a sure sign that this one could not be the Messiah. Yet the Gospels make clear how Jesus himself realized that his manner of impending death would subvert any expectation that he was the one for whom Israel waiting. In fact, that reversal of conventional expectations becomes a factor central to Jesus mission; as Messiah, if you will. Moreover, Jews could have attenuated the scandal by attending to the "suffering servant" narrative in Isaiah, as those who were attracted to Jesus would quickly do. For Muslims, however, with notable exceptions for the Prophet himself, the Qur'an seldom presents its exemplary figures as hesitant or "in the dark," as the sura Yusuf's portrayal of Jacob reveals. Biblical patriarchs, on the other hand, often miss the mark, as a way, it seems, of rendering all glory to God. So it would clearly be beneath the dignity of the "Word of God" (*kalimat Allah*) to be overpowered by pagans and crucified. Yet the elaborate ruses which some invent to "explain" so affronting an event seem utterly ad hoc, for the Qur'an simply says:

> ... and for their saying, "We slew the Messiah, Jesus son of Mary, the Messenger of God" – yet they did not slay him, neither crucified him, only a likeness of that was shown to them. ... they slew him not of a certainty, no, indeed; God raised him up to Him; God is All-mighty, All-wise. (4:155–160)[10]

The Qur'an's disclaimer about Jesus' death, however, carries far greater import than the dignity of one of the five messengers: Jesus, Noah, Abraham, Moses, and Muhammad.[11] It also critiques the Christian demand that the death of the Word of God (made human) would be required to gain human beings access to God's favor. We shall see this worked out in treating the Christen trope of "original sin." For the moment, it will suffice to call attention to the salient fact that "the crucified one" has no role to play in Muslim soteriology; Jesus' death is simply redundant to human beings' flourishing before God; a simple *yes* to the gift of the Qur'an and its message will suffice, as it calls believers to follow its "straight path."

How Can Christians Relate to Muslim Claims to a Fresh Revelation in Arabia Seven Centuries after Christ?

This final point is perhaps the most neuralgic, for it implicitly asks Christians whether they accept the Prophet (Muhammad) as God's prophet, and the Qur'an as God's revelation. Yet the most spontaneous Christian reaction to news of a fresh revelation in Arabia in the seventh century "after Christ" has to be repugnance; in short, an oxymoron. It is not that Christians fail to believe; it is rather that they fail to see how anyone could believe such a thing. We are driven back to the issue of chronological supersession, and the way the preceding religious tradition reacts to it. Jews often respond to the claims of Christians about Jesus with a simple: "we don't need it." In fact, however, all of those who initially followed Jesus in the wake of his death and with faith in his resurrection were Jews; as individual Jews throughout history have come to see that Jesus brought their Scriptures to an unprecedented focus. For the focus to which Jesus brings to the Scriptures, however formulated, does not stand in contradiction to those same Scriptures. There are even openings in the Scriptures themselves which Jesus would appear to fill, so a Jew attracted to Jesus could in fact appeal to his own revelation as making a way for that of Jesus. And Muslims will find similar openings in the Gospels, notably the verse in John which announces the advent of a mysterious "paraclete" who "will reveal to you everything which I have told you" (Jn 14:26).

Yet can Christians countenance Muslims exercising with regard to the New Testament the same logic they employ regarding "fulfilling" the Hebrew Scripture? The spontaneous answer has clearly been *no*, yet we must proceed to inquire whether the Qur'an can be said to be an authentic revelation of the same God whom Jews believe forged the first covenant with Moses, and whom Christians believe forged a new one in Jesus, or can lead us to appreciate the transcendence of a God made immanent to Christians in Jesus, and to Muslims in the Qur'an? And as the eminent Catholic Islamicist,

Roger Arnaldez, expounds in his engaging *Three Messengers for One God*, it is in the mystery of that one God that Abrahamic believers will be able to meet without losing their identity; rather, as experience abundantly shows, such encounters will bring each believer to a richer understanding of the gift of their respective revelations. Yet how can I, as a Catholic philosophical theologian, make a statement about the "respective revelations" of Christians and Muslims? My astute friend and interlocutor in Aberdeen, David Braine, insists that I cannot:

> I shall stick through thick and thin to my point, made not as a philosopher, not as a speculative theologian, but as something I understand to be integral to Catholic faith, namely: "I do not think that it is compatible with Christian doctrine that there be any new public revelation after the apostolic era" (communication of March 26, 2008).

And we would all agree, I am sure, that the one whom David Braine and I both acknowledge currently as Pope Benedict XVI would concur; as indeed the Christian community has consistently maintained since Islam emerged on the world scene. That explains, of course, why the most hospitable place Christians have been able to find for Islam was that of "a Christian heresy." Yet in a probing rather than a defensive spirit, can the initially offensive phrase "respective revelations of Christians and Muslims" be given a respectable theological pedigree?

Let me essay two examples which will not meet that challenge directly but may leave the door ajar. The first, and more familiar, notes the sea-change operated by the Vatican II document, *Nostra Aetate*, regarding the status of current Jews in the Christian imaginary. (I use "imaginary" to underscore that the position which the council replaced was never enshrined in church doctrine, however, widespread it may have been.) The extent of the official "about-face" can be illustrated by contrasting the Pauline text which the Council endorsed: "the gifts and the call of God are irrevocable" (Rom. 11:29), with the assertion of the letter to the Hebrews: "in speaking of a new covenant he treats the first as obsolete; and what is becoming obsolete and growing old is ready to vanish away" (8:13). Here conciliar authority implicitly invokes a strategy not unlike that employed in Qur'an interpretation (whereby certain texts "abrogate" others which appear to contradict them) to valorize the Romans text over that of Hebrews; though historians will remind us that the "supersessionist" image indicated by Hebrews had dominated the Christian imaginary to that point.

Debates over whether it remains appropriate to have "missions to the Jews," once the Church acknowledged the integrity of their call from God, were bound to ensue. Yet to contend, as the late Paul Van Buren was wont to do, that it would then be unseemly to claim that Jesus "fulfilled" the Hebrew Scriptures, seems to overreact to the old situation rather than respond to the new one inaugurated by *Nostra Aetate.* For however one may interpret the protean term, "fulfill," what it portends is enshrined in the Christian liturgical practice of Advent, underscoring how central to faith in Jesus is the contention that his presence brings the Hebrew Scriptures to an unparalleled and unprecedented focus, one sense of "fulfill." What the conciliar insistence on the integrity of God's call to Jews in the covenant would seem rather to demand of Christians is a respect for that initial covenant and for Jews currently abiding by it, even while celebrating its "fulfillment" in Jesus, so inviting Jews to give witness to that integrity in their lives and actions. Such a mutual respect for difference recalls the celebrated verse of the Qur'an:

> If God had so willed, He would have made you one community, but He wanted to test you through that which He has given you. So emulate each other in doing good, and God will judge about your differences. (5:48)

If our differences show one tradition to be superior to another in certain respects, and others to be superior to one's own in other respects, then what have we to say except to learn from one another?

In another key, the Qur'an's insistence that only "God will judge about your differences" should remind us that while engaging in dialog doubtless demands that we respect others' convictions about the truth of their revelation, we can afford to "bracket" the truth-question as we focus on the meaning of what they assert. In fact, neither adherents or interlocutors are in a position to assess the truth of a revelatory tradition, which is why doubt remains endemic, even to a faith which regards itself as "strong." Indeed, the very notion of a "strong faith" is freighted with paradoxes, as Paul reminds us again and again; and even in his bombastic stride in the Acts of the Apostles, Peter could hardly forget that fear of the Jewish power structure made him deny even knowing Jesus, so his mentor's darkest hour became his most shameful. The only way we have of discerning the truth (or falsity) of a religious tradition, it seems, is from its fruits. In our own personal lives, growing evidence of a spiritual power at work in us can lead to a progressive corroboration of a faith freely entered into and faithfully adhered to, though always imperfectly. Faith-claims, so-called, are so thoroughly hedged by paradoxes of this sort that it is difficult to speak of ascertaining the *truth* of a religious tradition. So it is only "right and just" for dialog to bracket such questions, and grant the faith-assertions of another while exploring their meaning, in an effort to probe the coherence and illuminate the life-giving character of another tradition, all the while anticipating that the exchange will also help us better to understand and appreciate our own. And that has certainly turned out to be the case in the experience of most who engage in interfaith dialog.

It may well be that characterizing dialog in that way also makes one sound non-committal, so confirming a polarity between *dialog* and *proclamation* that has marked some recent Roman and papal statements. But an act of proclaiming can at best be an act of witnessing; indeed, there is no other way to proclaim the truth of a faith-statement, short of stamping one's foot! (We used to ridicule erstwhile "Thomists" for their efforts not only to expound the philosophy but to prove that it was true! Again, how to do that but stamp one's foot?) These are hardly contentious points; they merely express the very grammar of faith. The truth (or falsity) of a religious tradition, then, is not open to our assessment; the best we can do is to attend to the witness given, and where that results in holy men and women (who are as recognizable to us all as "classics" are to a literary critic), then we have at hand the only evidence we can possibly have for the truth of a tradition. Wilfrid Cantwell Smith reminded us that any tradition which produces holy men and women deserves whatever respect we can give it, as being more than a human fabrication. Moreover, the Vatican II document *Lumen Gentium* ("Dogmatic Constitution on the Church") offers similar animadversions in the very context of discussing the church as "the people of God."

> Finally, those who have not yet received the Gospel are related in various ways to the people of God. In the first place we must recall the people to whom the testament and the promises were given and from whom Christ was born according to the flesh. On account of their fathers this people remains most dear to God, for God "does not repent of the gifts He makes nor of the calls He issues." But the plan of salvation also includes those who acknowledge the Creator. In the first place amongst these there are the Mohamedans [sic], who, professing to hold the faith of Abraham, along with us adore the one and merciful God, who on the last day will judge mankind. Nor is God far distant from those who in shadows and images seek the unknown God, for it is He who gives to all men life and breath and all things, and as Savior wills that all men be saved. Those also can attain to salvation who through no fault of their own do not know the Gospel of Christ or His Church, yet sincerely seek God and moved by grace strive by their deeds to do His will as it is known to them through the dictates of conscience. Nor does Divine Providence deny the helps necessary for salvation to those who, without blame on their part, have not yet arrived at an explicit knowledge of God and with His grace strive to live a good life. Whatever good or truth is found amongst them is looked upon by the Church as a preparation for the Gospel. She knows that it is given by Him who enlightens all men so that they may finally have life. (# 16)

This positive assessment of ways in which "other-believers" or even non-believers are already related to the Kingdom of God resonates with the Qur'an's insistence that "God will judge about your differences." By that same token, it firmly lays to rest any human query into "who can be saved," strongly implying that salvation (however we may understand it, and whatever it may be) is God's business; not ours! Yet have we not been skirting the vexing question: can the Qur'an be counted among "respective revelations?"

Indeed, we have, but in the interest of learning how to ask it properly. Yet by insisting (on logical grounds having to do with the nature of faith) that we are not in a position to answer the question one way or the other, it seems prudent to lay it to rest. But note that the question of the truth of Islamic revelation does not squarely parallel *Nostra Aetate*'s adoption of Paul's insistence regarding his own Jewish people that the "gifts and the call of God are irrevocable," for that enjoys scriptural warrant. (We must be careful to insert "Judaism" here, however, since that social construction is in fact younger than Christianity; what Paul is speaking of, and what Vatican II adopts, is the covenant faith of the people Israel, as lived out by contemporaries, some of whom currently confront the polemical anti-Christian dimensions of Judaism itself.) With Muslims, it seems the best we can do, doctrinally, is to consider them (as *Lumen Gentiium* does) included "in the first place [in] the plan of salvation" by the way they "acknowledge the Creator, ... profess to hold the faith of Abraham, [and] along with us adore the one and merciful God, who on the last day will judge mankind." The fact that these truths, for Muslims, derive from the Qur'an, does not by itself confirm the divine origin of the Qur'an, of course, but we have already insisted that no independent assessment can assure that, since adherence to Qur'an or Bible can only be by an act of faith. Yet everything points to extending respect to Muslims' faith in the Holy Qur'an, and doing so in such a way as to facilitate a radical change of attitude towards Muslims parallel with that effected towards contemporary Jews. To be sure, the grounds will be different, but the logical impossibility of saying either "yes" or "no" to the incisive question whether the Qur'an can be considered a revelation, together with the commendations of *Lumen Gentium*, as well as the way "ordinary Muslims" witness to a palpable sense of the presence of God in their lives, should all argue to the rightness (in the sense of a prudential judgment) of extending to them, as a community, respect for their faith in the Qur'an as revelation. This would represent a step beyond both *Lumen Gentium* and *Nostra Aetate*, which urged respect for Muslims but stopped short of acknowledging Islam as an inspired community, or *umma*. Yet the extension could be a quite natural one, for respecting people for their faith certainly entails respecting its source as they ascribe it.

Summary Reflections on these Neuralgic Issues

Whatever Western Christians may *think* about Judaism or Islam, it is their encounter with Jews and Muslims which will matter – to each person involved. It would be difficult to imagine a more deep-seated prejudice than that which perdured for centuries between European Christians and Jews – the "other" in their midst, to the point of some countries expelling them outright. Deadly proof of this prejudice can be found in the ease with which a neo-pagan Nazi regime could carry out its efficient plan of eliminating Jews – simply as Jews – from the very midst of traditionally Catholic countries. Moreover, the sea-change effected by Vatican II had to await the shared shame of the *Shoah* to be initiated, for as later Vatican reflections ("We Remember") acknowledged, a pervasive anti-Judaism had prevailed in the Christian West, and facilitated the Shoah there. The West was not long in finding another sinister "other" in "Soviet Communism," and when that evaporated in 1989, "Islam" emerged as a proven historical candidate. It seems that Hegel's analysis of the negative dynamics of nation-states was on target: each one needs a counterpart; Bertholdt Brecht opens "Mother Courage" with a recruiting sergeant announcing: "what we need is a good war!" So analyses like the ones I have attempted can offer little hope to countering something so irrational as the need for an "other," yet as the French love to remind us "les événements nous dépassent tous!"[12] So yet unexpected or untoward happenings may well open our hearts to the need for that very "other" to help correct what so many feel to be deeply errant in Western society, a drama superbly narrated in Charles Taylor's recent *A Secular Age*. In fact, one of those events – the response of 138 Muslim intellectuals to Pope Benedict and other Christian leaders, *A Common Word* – reminds us that such events are already taking place.[13]

Our analysis my best be concluded with images designed to illustrate the fundamental rapport between Muslims and Christians, turning on the complementary images of Qur'an and Jesus. We may begin with the image of Jesus as the "good shepherd" in John's Gospel:

> He calls his own sheep by name and leads them out. When he has brought out all his own, he goes ahead of them, and the sheep follow him because they know his voice; [for he comes] that they may have life, and have it abundantly. (Jn 10:3, 10)

Sheep, of course, are notoriously dumb! Yet their connection with the "good shepherd" is more instinctive than reflective, which I suspect to be the point of the parable. We are all "slow learners" when it comes to essential things, and especially things of God. Yet there is something within us which responds to an authentic voice: "Jesus spoke with authority; not as the scribes and Pharisees" – the gospel stand-in for any accredited religious teacher! And Peter's gloss on this text reminds us: "you were going astray like sheep, but now you have returned to the shepherd and guardian of your souls" (1 Pet. 2:25).

Linkages with the role the Qur'an plays in Islamic tradition are uncanny. The "inimitability" of the holy book is characteristically illustrated by the spontaneous effect it is said to have on Arabic speakers, so charmed by the rhythmic structure as to be drawn instinctively to its message. This recurrent fact reveals the *fitra* which all human beings share: the residual divine image in our faculties of apperception by which we can be drawn to the truth, despite countless distractions and self-serving denials. Moreover, to parallel Peter's comments (and echo a recurrent theme in John), Muslims name that "world" (*dunya*), which provides distraction and abets self-serving, the domain of ignorance(*jahiliyya*), recalling the situation which the Prophet encountered in the Hejaz when he began disseminating his revelation. This historical situation serves as a metaphor for the original human condition, in which we are all "going astray" until our hearts can acknowledge the revelation given: for Peter, "the shepherd and guardian of your souls"; for Muslims who frequently pray the opening sura of the Qur'an: "Guide us in the straight path, / The path of those whom you have blessed, / Not of those against whom there is displeasure, / Nor of those who go astray" (*al-Fatihah*).

Now what is required of those who hear the divine voice is to follow it; to obey its prompting (like sheep!), or (in one inadequate rendering of "Islam") to "submit" to its demands. As John puts it in response to a skeptical people asking: "What must we do to perform the works of God? This is the work of God, that you believe in him whom he has sent" (Jn 6:29). Notice once again that the focus is not on what Jesus says, but who Jesus is: from "you have the words of eternal life" to "you are the Word of eternal life." And it is instructive that Muslim tradition, at first distracted by the trenchant "distinction" between creator and creation, held the Qur'an to be created, as indeed everything which is not God must be. Yet before long, the very idea that God could be mute was seen to be unseemly, so it was asserted: the Qur'an itself must be uncreated, even though copies of it that we use will of course be created. A similar development took place in Judaism, with the "heavenly Torah" offering the model for God's creating. So both Torah and Qur'an are believed to be that Word "in the beginning with God," through which the universe is created and which, of course, must be intimately divine, since no multiplicity is to be tolerated in the One God. Here Christians will recall how that same demand, lodged in the *shema* ("hear, O Israel, God our God is One"), urged them to struggle to find the origins of their faith in Jesus as "one with God"; and certainly not a "being alongside God," thereby discovering prospective links with Muslim *tawhid*.

Notes

1 *Ascent of Mount Carmel* (Washington DC: Institute of Carmelite Studies, 1993), 2.22.

2 *Ignaz Maybaum: A Reader* (ed. Nicholas deLange; New York: Berghahn, 2001), p. 67.

3 *Common Word between Us* (www.acommonword.com/).

4 Dan Madigan, *The Qur'an's Self-Image: Writing and Authority in Islam's Scripture* (Princeton, NJ: Princeton University Press, 2001); *Al-Ghazali: The Ninety-Nine Beautiful Names of God* (trans. David Burrell and Nazih Daher; Cambridge: Islamic Texts Society, 1992; Louisville, KY: Fons Vitae, 1998).

5 Paul Griffiths, *Religious Reading: Practice of Reading in Religion* (Oxford: Oxford University Press, 1999).

6 For a succinct statement of the eternal Qur'an, see Kenneth Cragg's learned introduction to his *Readings in the Qur'an* (Portland, OR: Sussex Academic Press, 1999): "the Qur'an does not present itself as documenting what is other than itself. It is not about the truth; it is the truth … as a book already existing eternally" (p. 18); for an illuminating discussion, see Yahya Michot, "Revelation," in 'Iim Winter (ed.), *Cambridge Companion to Classical Islamic Theology* (Cambridge: Cambridge University Press, 2008), p. 185.

7 In Rik Van Nieuwenhove and Joseph Wawrykow (eds), *Theology of Thomas Aquinas* (Notre Dame, IN: University of Notre Dame Press, 2005).

8 Sebastian Moore, *The Crucified Jesus Is No Stranger* (Mahwah, NJ: Paulist Press, 1983).

9 See Kenneth Cragg, *Readings in the Qur'an*.

10 See Helmut Gätje, *The Qur'an and its Exegesis* (trans. and ed. Alford Welch; London: Routledge, 1971; Oxford: One World, 1997), 3.12, "The Death of Jesus," pp. 127–129.

11 Sachiko Murata and William Chittick, *The Vision of Islam* (Minneapolis, MN: Paragon House; London: IB Tauris, 1994), p. 134.

12 "Events blindside us all."

13 www.acommonword.com/; see Miroslav Volf, Prince Ghazi bin Muhammad bin Talal, Melissa Yarrington (eds), *A Common Word: Muslims and Christians on Loving God and Neighbor* (Grand Rapids, MI: Eerdmans, 2009).

Epilog

Misuses and Abuses of Abrahamic Traditions

Our approach to these three traditions has thus far been purpose-fully constructive, tracing how similarities and differences, con-verges and conflicts, have contributed to developments and can facilitate clarifications in each tradition. In part, this strategy responds to the new horizons offered by Vatican Council II in *Nostra Aetate*, as well as the startling rapprochement between Christianity and Islam in the wake of Pope Benedict's *felix culpa* in Regensburg. Yet it also stems from live appreciation of the inherently fruitful prospect of comparative theological inquiry, here inspiring bold engagement in a "creative hermeneutical" inquiry. Now to the blockages which have been in evidence in each of these traditions over the centuries – not to rehearse them, for such an exposition can lead literally to nausea; nor is it needed, since we are all sadly aware of these propensities in our respective traditions. But rather to offer a diagnosis: how do these multiple misuse and abuses of such promising revelational traditions arise? The short answer may well turn out to be the best: the God in question, whom each religious

Towards a Jewish-Christian-Muslim Theology, First Edition. David B. Burrell.
© 2011 John Wiley & Sons Ltd. Published 2011 by John Wiley & Sons Ltd.

family believes bestowed so remarkable a revelation on them, left it to them to elaborate. Jewish anecdotes in this vein abound: contentious parties demanding a *bat kol* (literally a "daughter of a voice") – a voice from heaven – to settle their dispute, do indeed hear a voice, only to admonish them: "I have left my Torah in the hands of my people to resolve." So it is with church and with *umma* as well. Can here be any wonder, then, that we have bowdlerized God's revelation to us? For God has deliberately left divine revelation in the hands of those afflicted with *yetzer ra* (the inclination to evil), or "original sin," or *jahiliyyah* (ignorance). The "ways of the Lord" are certainly inscrutable, yet less so when we reflect on the premium which this God we share places on human freedom.

Once in our hands, however, was it not inevitable that power and the lust for power would obscure the message with its messengers? We have seen how Jesus labored to subvert his people's expectations of a Messiah, to the point of submitting to an ignominious death at the hands of the power structures in Jerusalem. Yet as time progressed, neither Jesus' ostensible followers, nor later, Muslims who revered him, went to any lengths to avoid being contaminated by power. The two requirements Jesus had stipulated for entering the "kingdom of heaven" were that people acknowledge their transgressions to the point of asking forgiveness, and "become like little children." Neither of these comes naturally to those in power, and even when one is no longer powerful, their memoirs seldom acknowledge wrongdoing, even when it is manifest for all to see. (Like Genesis 3, the fault can only have been someone else's.) There have always been exemplary followers of Jesus, of course, or of Muhammad and Moses, as in the "ten just ones," poles around whom the universe turns, in Jewish and in Muslim lore, but the institutional leadership has too often been unrecognizable as Jewish, Christian, or Muslim, except in distinctive (and often ornate) dress. Until quite recently, Jews could escape this charge of hypocrisy linked to political power, but the 60-year experiment with a Jewish state in Israel has brought them full membership in this cadre of hypocrites who use religious tradition to justify horrors against humanity. As in each tradition, there are exemplary Israeli witnesses who protest this betrayal of the revelation, but most members of the clan resort to denial instead.[1] As have Christians for centuries, notably in staunch criticism of Muslim's holy book – the Qur'an – for licensing the use of force to establish an Islamic polity, while engaging in subterfuge to legitimize their own recourse to force – in the name of a Jesus who proscribed it! And so it goes: each tradition has been identified with leaders who are all too human, so relish power, yet besmirch their own tradition in seeking religious reasons to justify their recourse to power. Indeed, nothing better exemplifies Hannah Arendt's insight into the "banality of evil" than so-called "religious leaders" abusing the language of their revelatory traditions to indulge their own lust after power.

Yet mercifully, we can note how religious traditions themselves resist being identified with their visible leaders, by reminding onlookers that such an identification already represents a way of capitulating to the lust for power. This theme has been recurrent in these traditions from their beginnings, as faithful spontaneously turn to holy men or women for guidance, often bypassing institutional leadership. Hebrew prophets are esteemed as saints both in Christian and in Muslim tradition, for the ways they bring the revelation to life for other believers, often precisely by challenging power. So we might say that "hypocrites" are blessedly matched by "friends of God" in synagogue, church, and *umma*, so offering a clear rationale for the author of revelation to leave its unfolding to us, for without that radical freedom we could never have had bona fide friends of God. The document from Vatican Council II on the church, *Lumen Gentium*, deliberately engaged in a self-instruction to that very community, identifying it as "the people of God." To be sure, like any society, the church requires distinct components in a proper order but these do not constitute "the church" but rather constitute structures oriented to serve the people. Again, to be sure, some of those components will work assiduously to arrogate to themselves the title of "church," yet we have already come to identify power propensities, and others in the community can confront one more attempt to subvert Jesus' legacy. The same pattern is at work in each Abrahamic faith, negatively and positively: prominent members acceding to the lust for power, and others resisting that subversion of the revelation. And so it goes on, yet to wish that not to be the case would be to subvert in turn God's design of freedom, as Dostoevsky reminded us in his vignette of the "Grand Inquisitor" in *Brothers Karamazov*. For freedom is lodged at the heart of the Abrahamic journey of faith. Finally, religious traditions exercise their mission in this regard by constant self-criticism, as the history of multiple "reforms" exhibits. In fact, what distinguishes a religious tradition in principle from an ideology is precisely the demand of self-criticism, a demand generated by recurring revelatory transmissions. For an ideology cannot countenance self-criticism, and will regularly use force to prevent or to squelch it. So when a purported religious tradition acts in that way, it shows itself to be the opposite of what it is meant to be. But then we all know that the "corruption of the best is the worst." That is why systematic betrayal of a tradition by succumbing to the lust for power is so offensive even when it seems quite understandable.

Note

1   See Yeshayhu Leibowitz, *Judaism, Human Values, and the Jewish State* (ed. Eliezer Goldman; Cambridge, MA: Harvard University Press, 1992).

Index

Towards a Jewish-Christian-Muslim Theology, First Edition. David B. Burrell.
© 2011 John Wiley & Sons Ltd. Published 2011 by John Wiley & Sons Ltd.

Index

202